Black on Black

Urban Youth Films and the Multicultural Audience

Celeste A. Fisher

THE SCARECROW PRESS, INC.
Lanham, Maryland • Toronto • Oxford
2006

SCARECROW PRESS, INC.

Published in the United States of America
by Scarecrow Press, Inc.
A wholly owned subsidary of
The Rowman & Littlefield Publishing Group, Inc.
4501 Forbes Boulevard, Suite 200, Lanham, Maryland 20706
www.scarecrowpress.com

PO Box 317
Oxford
OX2 9RU, UK

Portions of the introduction, chapter 2, and chapter 6 were previously published and revised from "America's Worst Nightmare: Watching *Menace II Society* in a Culturally Diverse Setting," in *Say It Loud! Audiences, Media and Identity*, edited by Robin R. Means Coleman, 229–47. New York: Routledge, 2002.

British Library Cataloguing in Publication Information Available

Library of Congress Cataloging-in-Publication Data

Fisher, Celeste A.
  Black on black : urban youth films and the multicultural audience / Celeste A. Fisher.
    p. cm.
  Includes bibliographical references and index.
  ISBN-13: 978-0-8108-5722-3 (pbk. : alk. paper)
  ISBN-10: 0-8108-5722-7 (pbk. : alk. paper)
  1. African Americans in motion pictures. 2. Youth in motion pictures. I. Title.

PN1995.9.N4F57 2006
791.43'652996073—dc22

2005035444

To My Parents

Addie and Willie

Contents

~

Acknowledgments

I never could have imagined the impact of this project on my personal life or scholarly career. From the beginning, the work and the reaction of others to this work has been challenging, rewarding, and sometimes surprising. Early on, I had the opportunity to be surrounded by people who believed in it, and me, for which I am truly grateful. Through reading and questioning, they graciously shared their knowledge and time. For that, I am indebted to Christine Nystrom, Manthia Diawara, and Joy Gould Boyum for their guidance during the process of design, writing, and revision. Their insights were invaluable. For an earlier design of this project, Marie Fortini, Rataa McCrae, and Ellen Frisina assisted me with fieldwork that, although not presented here, had a significant impact on my present work. I owe them my thanks, as well as to Dominique Annoual and Carlos Greer, who helped me during the final hours. I am also grateful to Stephen Ryan for his comments during the final stages of this project and helping me to pull it all together and to my students, who willingly gave of themselves in the classroom, keeping me current and challenging my notions of popular culture, as only they can. On a more personal level, it is difficult to express in words how extremely thankful I am for my parents, Willie Fisher and

Addie Fisher, and my brothers, Victor and Derek. Their understanding and encouragement got me through the day. It would not have been the same or meant as much without them. Finally, I am truly grateful for my friend Johnny K. Newkirk, who phoned every day, just to make me laugh. His spirit will always be with me.

~

Introduction

After gaining permission from the Board of Education to conduct research involving urban high school students in the public school system, I thought that I was well on my way to understanding how teenagers respond and make meaning of what some would call "ghetto-centric street films" or "hood films." My initial goal was to have students at two high schools in the northeastern part of the United States screen three films. After viewing each film, they were to discuss what they had seen with other members in their selected group. Participation was strictly voluntary and did not interfere with normal classroom instruction. All screenings and their subsequent discussions were to take place after school or during free periods. Urban high school students seemed an appropriate population for this research because they are part of the target audience for hood films. For the purposes of this study, the composition of the audience was also of great importance. As such, I wanted to ensure that black male youths, who were not only the subjects of the films but also the subject of debate—given the violent incidents that occurred throughout the country during the theatrical release of some of these films—were represented.

Over the course of several months, I contacted several secondary school principals about the possibility of having their students screen a few films and then talk about them in groups. Although some administrators were receptive at first, their responses soon changed after I told them what films were included in the study. Most of the principals I talked to admitted that they had never seen a hood film. So I often found myself trying to assure them that each student's parents would be required to sign a permission slip and that, based on my experience, many of the students had already seen the films. Routinely, I was told that they did not think that showing the films would be a "good idea." While these rejections were somewhat disappointing, I must admit, their denial only fueled my interest in the subject.

Ultimately, I was successful in obtaining access to two high schools. But I decided that in order to reach my research goals, I had to shift the population of the study (slightly modifying my research focus and design) to college students since the schools for which I was allowed access did not possess the cultural diversity that I desired. While the responses of urban high school students would have, most likely, been different from the slightly older, more educated college students described in this study, college students are still part of the target audience for the films and, as such, bring their own unique backgrounds and experiences to the interpretation of texts.

Clearly, images of violent black masculinity are not new in American culture. Their production and consumption has always created some form of public debate. Recently, however, the social and economic climate in the country that contributed to the production of ghetto life in cinema during the late 1980s and early 1990s was instrumental in pushing social and economic issues into the forefront of the American consciousness. The number of films produced on urban ghetto life at that particular point in time created profit for some and uneasiness for others. While Hollywood profited, the country was in the midst of an ever-widening "opportunity gap" between marginalized groups and mainstream society as well as an increase in juvenile violence.[1] These events added to the country's awkwardness in viewing, let alone engaging in, dialogue regarding representations of young black males living in urban ghettos.

Ghettocentric Youth Film

In July 1991, Columbia Pictures released *Boyz n the Hood*, written and directed by twenty-three-year-old filmmaker John Singleton. Singleton, a product of South-Central Los Angeles and the University of Southern California film school, made *Boyz* for about $6 million. The low-budget drama about ghetto life proved to be a good investment for Columbia. The film opened third at the box office for the weekend behind Tri-Star's big-budget action film *Terminator 2: Judgment Day* and Disney's re-release of the 1961 animated classic *101 Dalmatians*. *Terminator 2* (which cost $102 million to make) went on to gross over $204.8 million during its theatrical release, making it the number one film for the year. *Boyz n the Hood* (which showed on far fewer screens) ranked nineteenth for the year, earning $57.5 million during its theatrical release—more than nine times what it cost to make.[2] *Boyz*, however, was more than just a commercial success; it also garnered critical acclaim. The film received several honors, including two Academy Award nominations for best screenplay and best director.[3] Roger Ebert of the *Chicago Sun-Times* wrote that it was "not simply a brilliant directorial debut, but an American film of enormous importance."[4]

The commercial and critical success of *Boyz n the Hood* in 1991 helped to create a place in Hollywood for the black underclass. Films such as *Straight Out of Brooklyn* (1991), *Juice* (1992), *Menace II Society* (1993), *Poetic Justice* (1993), *Just Another Girl on the I.R.T.* (1993), *Clockers* (1995), and *Set It Off* (1996) soon followed. Unlike Dennis Hopper's *Colors* (1988), starring Robert Duval and Sean Penn, which examined gang life in South-Central Los Angeles from a cop's point of view, ghettocentric hood films painted a portrait of the marginalized individuals who make up underclass African American communities.

With the exception of *Just Another Girl on the I.R.T.*, directed by Leslie Harris, and a few films by nonblack directors (e.g., *Fresh*, Boaz Yakin; *South Central*, Steve Anderson), hood films are primarily the products of black male filmmakers. According to Manthia Diawara, the genre was generated out of black male masculinity—young black men coming of age in a hostile urban environment where knowledge of the streets is essential to their survival.[5] The characters live in impoverished neighborhoods where drugs and gang activity are a way of life. Many come from single-parent homes where the father is rarely visible. In the "New Ghetto Aesthetic," Jacquie Jones notes that women in this genre generally occupy supporting roles, ranging from strong yet flawed single mothers to crack addicts. More often than not, they are referred to as "bitches" and "hos."[6]

As a whole, black-on-black crime and distrust of police are common themes in hood films. Other themes in the genre include revenge (e.g., *Boyz n the Hood*), a boy's initiation into manhood (e.g., *Juice*), and the struggle to escape one's surroundings (e.g., *Straight Out of Brooklyn*).[7] With few exceptions, characters exhibit a feeling of helplessness and hopelessness (e.g., *Menace II Society*) as well as a need to survive their current conditions by adapting to the laws of the streets (e.g., *Juice, Set It Off*). Many of the films are set on the West Coast, which has been the focus of highly publicized gang activity. For the most part, the sound tracks for hood films are dominated by rap music, an art form also dominated by black men that reflects issues of importance to black male, urban youth.

One of the reasons that the audiences for hood films are so important in the public sphere is directly related to the types of stories told about black urban underclass communities. As such, the most controversial aspect of hood films is, arguably, the representation of the urban environment. The neighborhood, which is typically set in Los Angeles, consists of dilapidated buildings and noisy, overcrowded housing projects. It is a place where drug use, unemployment, and single-parent families are commonplace. While there are "decent" people who live in the hood, they are generally elderly people who appear to lack the means to move or the ability to change things (*Boyz n the Hood* and *Menace II Society*). Therefore, its inhabitants establish their own laws and have their own sense of morality.

The neighborhoods in hood films are constructed as separate from the city in which they are located. They are culturally and economically isolated from the diversity in the rest of the city. This is evidenced by the lack of white characters in many of the films. Whiteness is marginalized.[8] Nearly invisible, it is generally used to provide a context for the conditions that exist in the neighborhood. When explicit, it usually takes the form of policing. Similarly, the presence of an educated, black middle class is almost nonexistent (except for characters such as Furious Styles in *Boyz n the Hood* who choose to live in the hood).[9]

However dismal the depiction of black life, in the early 1990s, ghettocentric street films generated a great deal of money at the box office. *Boyz n the Hood* took in $10 million in its first weekend.[10] As a result, some scholars have credited hood films with helping to revitalize the film industry and starting the second black movie boom since the early 1970s.[11] But the financial success of the two genres and the utilization of predominantly black casts are where the similarities end when comparing these two eras in filmmaking.

The blaxploitation films that emerged shortly after the civil rights movement were essentially fantasy films—directed primarily by white directors. The genre placed importance on the role of individuals on the fringes of society by depicting a "super black"—or lone hero who challenged dominate culture and won (e.g., *Superfly*).[12] What scholars such as Ed Guerrero refer to as "the second wave of blaxploitation films," however, is somewhat different. The more recent films are coming-of-age stories in which the characters struggle to define themselves in relationship to the environment in which they live. As a result, the principal characters are younger—generally teenage boys embroiled in intragroup conflicts (i.e., black-on-black crime) that are sometimes linked to racism in mainstream American society (e.g., *Boyz n the Hood*, *Menace II Society*). The protagonists exist in an environment that perpetuates criminality (e.g., *Juice* and *Set It Off*). Loyalty to one's peer group is, more often than not, central to the plot. Finally, "realism" and the desire to graphically depict that realism are defining characteristics of the new wave of blaxploitation films.[13]

But by the mid-1990s, the wave of new films was, for all intents and purposes, over. The subsequent end of this period in cinematic history in the mid-1990s has been attributed to its failure to create a diversity of images, settings, and themes.[14] In other words, people just got tired of watching. Evidence of this is illustrated by the theatrical release of *Don't Be a Menace to South Central while Drinking Your Juice in the Hood* (1996), a parody of hood films. It can also be argued, however, that much like the films of the first wave, they are no longer needed by Hollywood to boost box office receipts. Nevertheless, the genre continues to be the subject of debate because it illuminates the concerns of the black urban underclass and the fears of the white majority.

Crossover Appeal

One of the most interesting aspects of the films is the audience that they attract. Although hood films and rap music in general focus clearly on the lives of black youth in urban environments, they also appeal to other ethnic, racial, and socioeconomic groups. Aside from press interviews and television advertisements (which reach an extremely large nondifferentiated group of viewers), one can look to the theatrical trailers and promotional posters for hood films as evidence of what can attract nonblack movie audiences to the films. These promotional tools offer potential movie audiences, by virtue of their placement in the movie theater, a brief glimpse into a film's narrative. The status of rap music in American society, a general cultural attraction to violent images, and the influence of various genres in which race and ethnicity create culturally specific (albeit stereotypical) representations of "foreign" spaces helped to shape the genre and its promotional materials and thus the audience for such films.

Theatrical trailers for hood films often feature rap music as well as rap artists as actors within the narrative. It is this aspect of the films that plays a major role in their crossover appeal. S. Craig Watkins points out that the ability of the films to reach more mainstream audiences is linked to the introduction of rap videos on MTV—a move made primarily for the purpose of increasing its sagging viewership. He goes on to state that "the ability of rap music to crossover into a broader sphere of youth consumption was crucial to its eventual absorption into other arenas of popular cultural production,"[15] including film. As such, the crossover appeal of rap music was instrumental in attracting nonblack audiences to hood films because the films were, for the most part, an extension of the rap video.[16] But to understand the attraction of hood films for mainstream audiences, one must also have at least a general understanding of the attraction of rap music for nonblack and/or middle-class listeners. Tricia Rose argues that there is a certain value attributed to rap music that attracts white participants and audience members—not unlike other black musical genres such as jazz, rock 'n' roll, soul, and rhythm and blues. She contends that young white listeners of black music are trying to "perfect a model of correct white hipness, coolness, and style by adopting the latest black style and image."[17]

Rap artists drive the sound tracks for many of the films and occupy central roles as actors in the genre—Ice Cube in *Boyz n the Hood*, Tupac Shakur in *Juice* and *Poetic Justice*, and Queen Latifah in *Set It Off*, for example. They appear in the promotional posters for the films—either visually or as part of the text—and in the theatrical trailers. Potential audiences interested in rap and attracted to its representation in music videos would therefore be interested in films in which various rappers and rap music are featured.

These popular images of young black men in America are extremely complex in that they are both attractive (as a standard for what is hip and cool) and feared. It stands to reason, then, that the construction of black youth in hood films has attracted some would-be moviegoers who are not necessarily interested in rap but are curious about that particular construction of black masculinity. In the 1980s and 1990s specifically, negative representations of young black men were pervasive in mainstream news and entertainment. According to William L. Van Deburg, the media's fascination with gang life played a significant role in normalizing the image of young gang members wreaking havoc on society.[18] Films such as *Boyz n the Hood* provided a view of the ghetto from the perspective of the young black men who reside in these communities. For some mainstream audience members, the uniqueness of this experience was undoubtedly part of the genre's appeal.[19] Hood films added greater depth to the image of violent black youth that appeared in the news. In some ways, it explained conditions and ways of life in segregated urban communities to the mainstream while situating viewers in the relative comfort of a movie theater. A critic for the *Los Angeles Times* wrote, "What *Boyz n the Hood* . . . does best is present a convincing panoply of life as it is lived in South-Central L.A. Like a jazz ensemble, Singleton and his actors slowly involve us in an almost sensual mélange of moods, images and situations that take us inside the ghetto in a way mainstream films almost never do."[20]

Other Genres

In looking at the theatrical trailers, it is clear that hood films are class and/or culturally specific in terms of location (black ghettos), colloquial speech, and, to some extent, behavior (gang life). The films, however, also bear some semblance to other genres. The influence of gangster and kung fu films, in particular, played key roles in creating a diverse audience for the films. Anyone with some familiarity with the conventions of these genres would have entry into the world of the cinematic urban ghetto because they would already be familiar with its narrative formula.

Gangster films, in particular, had a huge impact on hood films because of their focus on ethnicity, which, according to Todd Boyd, was substituted for race in ghettocentric street films. Popular films such as *The Godfather* (1972) and *Scarface* (1983) are highly stylized representations of mob life. Aside from an unquestionable loyalty to "family" similar to that seen among gang members in hood films, they construct violent, aggressive, and chauvinistic definitions of masculinity. Women in gangster films play secondary roles, much like the women in hood films.[21] These narrative constructions have had a profound influence on hip-hop culture, in general, as expressed in its music, fashion, and film.

While the influence of gangster films is rather apparent, the narrative for hood films has also received inspiration from Asian kung fu cinema of the 1970s. As cultural critic Nelson George states,

> The youth culture of aggression that hip-hop has codified (and commodified) also has roots in kung fu flicks. Parallel to blaxploitation coming out of Hollywood was an influx of films from Hong Kong and Asia that, for a time, replaced Westerns as the grassroots morality plays of the age. Based on a rigid formula similar to films like *Shane* as well as Asian folktales, these kung fu flicks tend to center on a virtuous yet humble martial arts initiate called upon to seek revenge against some evil clan that has caused injury to his family, teacher, school, or village.[22]

The youth culture of aggression to which George is referring is embodied in American culture in general and as such consumes a large amount of cinematic space. American audiences are hugely attracted to graphic, physical violence in films as portrayed in a variety of genres. Not surprisingly, violent images play a prominent role in many of the theatrical trailers and promotional posters for mainstream films. A number of the top grossing films of all time are extremely violent. From the late 1980s to the early 1990s, when hood films were at their peak, films such as *Lethal Weapon 2* (1989), *Die Hard 2* (1990), *The Silence of the Lambs* (1991), *Terminator 2: Judgment Day* (1991), *Lethal Weapon 3* (1992), *Pulp Fiction* (1994), *True Lies* (1994), and *Se7en* (1995) spoke to an enormous appetite for violent imagery in American culture.[23] It is therefore reasonable to conclude that the attraction to violent images in mainstream society naturally extends to include the potential audience for films that focus on the lives of black urban youth, although the representation of violence varies significantly from genre to genre.[24]

In addition to the film genres mentioned earlier, there are several somewhat overlooked films produced in Hollywood during the 1970s that were either directed, written, and/or based on literary works by blacks and that have since gained cult status, which, while not directly contributing to the cross-cultural appeal of hood films, have influenced a generation of hip-hop recording artists, including Lauryn Hill, Boyz II Men, and Wu-Tang Klan,[25] as well as filmmakers from this generation— consciously and unconsciously.

Urban Youth Films of the 1970s

In the early part of the decade, there were two films that focused on the lives of rural black youth—*The Learning Tree* (1969), directed by famed photographer Gordon Parks, and *Sounder*, released in 1972, for which Lonnie Elders III wrote the screenplay. But while black youth navigated the Southern terrain of a bygone era in the earliest part of the decade, the cinematic cities belonged to the hustlers of the blaxploitation era—attracting large numbers of black moviegoers seeking images of black people who have the ability to effect change within the urban environment in which they live. Following suit, black male coming-of-age films turned their attention to city life. Like the great migration of blacks from the South to the North, a modern urban society was seen to possess more economic and educational opportunities. However, in films focusing on black urban youth, that did not turn out to be the case.

In 1974, *The Education of Sonny Carson* was released. Sometimes referred to as blaxploitation, the film tells the story of troubled Brooklyn youth turned civil rights activist, Sonny Carson. The film, based on his autobiography, is a gritty and disturbing depiction of a boy's transition from honor student to career criminal during the 1950s. In one of the most graphic scenes in the film, Carson (Rony Clayton) receives a horrific beating by a police officer while he is chained to the wall in the basement of a police precinct. Later, his experiences in prison, as well as seeing his friends die of gang violence and drug overdoses, help him to realize that he must turn his life around. The theme of the film, according to critics, is that of survival.

Although the film was generally not well received by the press, it is important in black coming-of-age cinema because it takes a look at gang life in a ghetto environment—which is significant in its influence on contemporary images of the hood. If the blaxploitation films of the time played a major role in defining modern black communities in urban spaces (no matter how exaggerated they were), then *The Education of Sonny Carson* provided audiences with a graphic look at coming of age in such an environment. For authenticity, Carson served as technical director for the film using real gang members, prisoners, and community residents.

The following year, two other coming-of-age films were released: *Cooley High* and *Cornbread, Earl & Me* (1975). *Cornbread, Earl & Me* is based on the novel *Hog Butcher* by Ronald L. Fair, an African American writer from Chicago. In the film, it is clear from the narrative how a boy becomes a man. Wilford (Larry Fishburne III) is called to testify in a trial that will convict a police officer for accidentally shooting his friend and star basketball player Cornbread (Keith Wilkes), who is going off to college. The hope of the community dies with Cornbread—at least initially. Since the police have intimidated witnesses, including beating and threatening his mother, the whole case rests on Wilford. In the courtroom, Wilford's mother (Rosalind Cash) tells him explicitly that if he tells the truth, he is a man and will always be a man. At the end of the film, we see Wilford teaching his younger friend Earl (Tierre Turner) how to play basketball, just like Cornbread had taught him. The lesson learned is that boys become men by standing up for what is right and teaching others.

The comedy/drama *Cooley High* (1975) is perhaps the more popular of the two films.[26] Written by Eric Monte and directed by Michael Schultz, the film is set on the South Side of Chicago in 1964. *Cooley High* tells the story of a group of black teenage boys whose lives change forever after two of them (Preach, played by Glynn Turman, and Cochise, played by Lawrence-Hilton Jacobs III) take a joyride with a couple of drug dealers. After their teacher, Mr. Mason (Garrett Morris), gets them out of jail, Cochise, the star basketball player who has just received a college scholarship, is killed by the drug dealers who believe that they have been sold out to the police. From the written narration at the end of the film, the audience learns that Preach moves to Hollywood and becomes a successful screenwriter and that the drug dealers are killed during an armed robbery. In this film, boys learn life lessons by rebelling against authority and testing boundaries (skipping school, having sex in their parents' house, smoking marijuana, and so on).

In 1978, audiences were introduced to a film adaptation of Alice Childress's novel A Hero Ain't Nothin' but a Sandwich. Childress, who also wrote the screenplay, tells the story of Benjie (Larry B. Scott), a thirteen-year-old heroin addict living in South-Central Los Angeles. In the film, Benjie lives with his mother Sweets (Cicely Tyson); his mother's companion Butler (Paul Winfield), a maintenance worker; and his grandmother. In several scenes, we are led to believe that Benjie's drug use is linked to his father's abandonment. And although Butler tries to be a father figure, Benjie rebels. Butler makes the point that "celebrities aren't heroes. People who get up every day and go to regular jobs are heroes." But Benjie's dissent is fueled by his need to escape his environment, his life. He thinks that drugs and death are the only way out. By the end of the film, Benjie agrees to get help for his addiction. A still shot of Benjie and Butler hugging and smiling fills the screen as the credits unfold. The narrative most clearly articulates the importance of fathers in children's lives but does not claim that little black boys will live to grow into men.

Working-class black communities dominated the urban youth films of the 1970s. Parents held low-paying jobs and tried to instill in their children certain values, like hard work and getting an education. Various levels of violence and drug use are a part of growing up (The Education of Sonny Carson, A Hero Ain't Nothin' but a Sandwich, and Cooley High). Alienation (A Hero Ain't Nothin' but a Sandwich), police brutality and corruption (The Education of Sonny Carson and Cornbread, Earl & Me), and the desire to escape one's surroundings (Cooley High, A Hero Ain't Nothin' but a Sandwich, and Cornbread, Earl & Me) were common themes. Like the blaxploitation films of the time, several of these films focused on the individual experience (e.g., The Education of Sonny Carson and A Hero Ain't Nothin' but a Sandwich) of urban living.

Whiteness is also marginalized—often presented as authority figures. But despite some of these themes, most of the films left the audience with a sense of hope for the future—regardless of the harsh conditions in which the characters live.

There are clearly some similarities in the ghettocentric youth films of the 1970s and the hood films of the 1990s. Aside from the fact that these are all essentially coming-of-age films, the narratives, for instance, are quite similar. The main overriding theme is that of escape—particularly the notion that one must or wants to break away from his current environment in order to survive, to be successful, or even to change it. The ghetto is not safe, even for those striving to make a better life for themselves. Although there is a sense of hopelessness in the community, the residents in these films struggle to find ways to survive and dream of ways to get out. While college sports scholarships (*Boyz n the Hood*, *Cooley High*, and *Cornbread, Earl & Me*) are sometimes seen as viable, positive options to better their condition, they seldom work—as star athletes are killed in violent ways.

Another important theme relates to who bears responsibility for the conditions that exist in the hood. The urban environment, as it is constructed, breeds criminality—the cause of which is most clearly attributed to the dominant culture but fostered by the unwitting participation of the residents in the community (*Boyz n the Hood*, *Menace II Society*, *The Education of Sonny Carson*, and *A Hero Ain't Nothin' but a Sandwich*). Isolation, "white policing of black populations," and the availability of illegal drugs are some of the factors that contribute to the condition of black neighborhoods.[27] Urban youth films of the 1970s and 1990s, overall, however, suggest that in order to increase the number of positive outcomes for local youth, more community involvement is needed.

Theatrically released films produced during the 1970s focusing on black urban youth, like the hood films that followed, sparked social concern and debate. With the exception of *Cooley High*, these films, overall, received little attention by the mainstream press compared to earlier youth films examining rural life. The relative lack of critical reviews in mainstream newspapers throughout the United States suggests that the issues/themes the films addressed, as well as their target audience, were not of major concern to the larger society. Urban youth films of the 1970s generally lacked crossover interest. Out of the films that focused on black urban youth, *Cooley High* had the most universal appeal. A critic from *Newsweek* wrote, "The separate but equal doctrine functions very well in the case of *Cooley High*, a spirited companion piece to *American Graffiti*."[28]

Black film critics expressed a variety of positions on black cast films of the time. Some talked about black films as social commentary, emphasizing the great importance placed on the images produced. The opening paragraph of an article in *Ebony* magazine about *The Education of Sonny Carson*, for instance, describes life in the ghetto for "the many thousands of black children" before discussing the film.[29] Critic James P. Murray wrote about the types of black films being made and the audiences that they attract. Murray's article titled "Lurid Movie Boom Over, but Blacks Films Steady On" in *Variety* celebrates the end of the blaxploitation era and the emergence of films with more crossover appeal such as *Cooley High* and *Cornbread, Earl & Me*.[30] Yet another critic expressed a desire for more multidimensional representations of blacks in cinema. In her review of *A Hero Ain't Nothin' but a Sandwich*, Angela E. Smith, writing for the *New York Amsterdam News* comments, "We, who have been raising cane because of the poor quality of films depicting Black life, should rejoice, this film is about as close as we'll get to a realistic portrayal of ghetto life in relation to Black youngsters."[31]

While there are clearly some narrative and aesthetic differences in the films of the 1970s and the 1990s (such as an emphasis on gang life in the latter decade), they illustrate that the concern about responses to particular constructions of blackness, specifically representations of black urban youth, is not a new debate. Acts of violence, associated with the theatrical screening of films in the hood genre, are.

Meaning-Making Responses

One of the major topics of concern in the study of communication and culture is the nature of the relationship between media and their audiences—that is, how the structures of different media and their contents affect the meaning-making responses of "readers" to texts of different kinds and how the characteristics of different "readers" also shape response in the transactions between readers and texts. In recent years, a growing body of scholarship in reader-response theory has begun to examine the role of texts, readers, and context in shaping the meaning-making responses of audiences to narratives. The largest proportion of reader-response scholarship to date has examined differences in the responses of different readers to written literary texts.[32] With the growth of the audiovisual media and the increasing centrality of such media as television and film in the American ecology of communication, however, audiovisual "texts" have come to serve as a major source of narrative, particularly for the young. Only a small number of researchers to date, however, have applied the insights, principles, and questions of reader-response theory and scholarship to the study of "readers'" responses to the narratives constructed in television and film. Two such studies, Liebes and Katz's *The Export of Meaning: Cross-Cultural Readings of* Dallas and Morley's *The Nationwide Audience*, have called attention in particular to the role that such differences among "readers" as their cultural identification play in shaping responses to narrative television texts.[33] And a small number of studies of the audiences for movie narratives and their responses has also indicated that such differences among "readers" of films as gender and cultural background are significant in shaping meaning making and response.[34] Indeed, it is by now widely accepted, among both reader-response theorists in literary studies and among "audience" theorists in cultural studies, that meaning making is a social process—that is, that the transactions between individual readers and texts occur within and are inescapably influenced by institutionalized relations of power.[35] Contemporary studies of "readers'" responses to audiovisual media like television, therefore, have given close attention to the individual "reader's" situation within such social contexts as neighborhood, peer group, home, school, and family and have shed light on the ways in which such personal "situations" affect readers' transactions with texts.[36] Such studies, however, have largely examined meaning making as an individual psychological process occurring *within* social settings and institutions.

The study I report here was designed to explore a different aspect of the role of "immediate social context" in the meaning-making process. Specifically, I examine the idea that meaning can in some instances be an intrapsychic event occurring between readers and texts within social and cultural contexts and a dynamic *interpersonal* process—that is, that meaning can be constructed, at least in some cases, during its expression to specific others in dialogue and that the dynamics of the dialogue and the relations among the participants play a major role in the meanings readers give to texts. To my knowledge, this idea has not been systematically explored in other studies of meaning making, although researchers such as Liebes and Katz have noted the impact of the interpersonal dynamics in their response groups on the participants' expression of meanings. (Liebes and Katz mention this only briefly as an artifact of their research design that may have "distorted" their findings on the meanings different audiences give to a television program.) To explore the role of immediate social context in meaning making, I tape-recorded and analyzed the group discussions of approximately fourteen college undergraduates of diverse cultural backgrounds, in a classroom setting, in response to three popular ghettocentric "street" or "hood" films of the 1990s.

Ghettocentric "street" films (*Boyz n the Hood*, *Menace II Society*, and *Juice*) were chosen as the "texts" for this study for three reasons. First, these films generated a variety of different responses from audiences of different sociocultural backgrounds when they were originally released and thus seemed likely to generate a variety of different meanings to be "negotiated" in a culturally diverse classroom. Second, the reaction of audiences to the films at the time of their release highlighted the questions of this study—that is, questions about the roles played in audiences' meaning making and response by the "messages" in "the text itself," the experiences audiences bring to the text, the sociocultural "situation" of different audiences, and the immediate social context in which meanings and responses are constructed. At the time of their theatrical showing, these films became a focus of widespread social concern and debate because of the outbreaks of violence among some young people that accompanied the viewing of such films in neighborhood theaters.[37] While some mainstream critics blamed the films for the reaction of some audience members, the writers and producers of films like *Boyz n the Hood* (which was followed by such an outbreak of violence) have for the most part denied responsibility for such responses by young people, arguing that their films were intended to communicate prosocial messages and did not suggest, endorse, or support violence as a response to the urban ghetto problems they depict.[38] Some cultural critics suggested that the life experiences of the viewers were the major factor in generating anti-social responses among some audiences. Many film executives argued, on the other hand, that the antisocial responses were the product of the immediate viewing situation and the dynamics of large groups. In short, these films brought to urgent popular attention and debate the questions about meaning making and response that are the focus of this study. They seemed a particularly apt set of "texts," therefore, for studying those questions in a more controlled context.

Chapter 1, "Readers and Response," provides the theoretical framework for the study, which shifts the focus of current research on hood films from the larger social context to the immediate social context.[39] It also describes the protocol and the method of data analysis—detailing how subjects were recruited for participation (enrollment in a class on contemporary black cinema) as well as their socioeconomic class status and race/ethnicity (information self-reported in a back-ground questionnaire).

Chapters 2 through 4 provide an examination of participant responses to each film under study (i.e., *Menace II Society, Juice,* and *Boyz n the Hood*). For each chapter, I provide a summary of the narrative for the film being discussed. The next section is a discussion of the verbal response strategies used by participants in dialogue following each film. Of particular importance are those who significantly influenced the flow of the conversation, the tone of the discussions, and the themes that characterized the discussion.

The title for chapter 2, "'America's Worst Nightmare': Reading *Menace II Society,*" was adapted from a line in the film spoken by the character Caine, in reference to his friend O-Dog. It, I believe, sums up the intent of the filmmaker. What is significant about the chapter on *Menace II Society* is that it illustrates how the participants focused their attention on the world outside the film and how emotionally charged their discussion was. Participants clearly articulated their subject-position and discussed how it related to what they believed. They talked about the film as though they were "objective viewers" and judged the film on its "reality" or "authenticity," arguing that others would perceive it as such.

The title of chapter 3, "'Money, Power, Respect': Reading *Juice*," also addresses the theme of the film. It is adapted from a song by The Lox, featuring DMX & Lil' Kim. *Juice*, the second film viewed by participants in the hood genre, was different with regard to its narrative and viewer responses. The focus of this discussion was on the aesthetics of the film and the construction of the narrative in an attempt to understand whether it was a good or bad film. From this, participants generally seemed concerned about the film's believability. Although several of the participants struggled with the construction of the film for a variety of reasons, the film's aesthetics was clearly of concern to theater executives. Their concern regarding violence was so significant that the gun (which appeared in the original promotional poster) was airbrushed out.

Chapter 4, "'Increase the Peace': Reading *Boyz n the Hood*," is also taken from the film itself, reflecting the intent of the filmmaker. While discussing the last film in the hood genre, participants appeared calmer than in previous discussions—in the way that they addressed one another and talked about the film. They were very much interested in the success of the individual characters in achieving their goal (making it out of the ghetto). They were emotionally moved and connected to the experiences of the characters.

Chapter 5, "Negotiated Meanings," summarizes the role of the films in shaping response, the role of the reader in shaping response, and the role of the immediate social context in shaping response for the three films under study. Further, it explains how the questions for the study were confirmed in that the immediate social context (i.e., the composition of the group) has a significant impact on how images are interpreted.

Chapter 6, "Epilogue," provides an overview of the study and examines the implication of the research findings. It also situates the study within reader-response criticism, the theoretical framework on which this research is based. Finally, I explore the implications for the study and provide a suggestion for future research.

Notes

1. Ed Guerrero, *Framing Blackness: The African American Image in Film* (Philadelphia: Temple University Press, 1993), 159, and Keith Bradsher, "America's Opportunity Gap," *New York Times*, June 4, 1995, sec. 4, 1.

2. The weekend of July 12–14, *Terminator 2: Judgment Day* (which opened on July 3) was shown on 2,289 screens across the country. The movies *101 Dalmatians* and *Boyz n the Hood* opened during the same weekend on 1,777 and 829 screens, respectively. *Boyz n the Hood* had a prescreen average of $12,091, higher than *Terminator 2* at $9,060 for that weekend. The prescreen average for *101 Dalmatians* was $5,784. Source: variety.com.

3. The film received several awards: the BMI Film Music Award, the Image Award for Outstanding Motion Picture, the MTV Movie Award for Best New Filmmaker, the New York Film Critics Circle Award for Best New Director, the Political Film Society Award for Peace, and the Young Artist Award for Outstanding Young Ensemble Cast in a Motion Picture. Source: imdb.com.

4. Roger Ebert, "Brilliant *Boyz n the Hood* Combines Substance, Style," *Chicago Sun-Times*, July 12, 1991.

5. Manthia Diawara, "Black American Cinema: The New Realism," in *Black American Cinema*, ed. Manthia Diawara (New York: Routledge, 1993), 3–25.

6. Jacquie Jones, "The New Ghetto Aesthetic," *Wide Angle* 13, nos. 3 and 4 (July–October 1991): 34.

7. Diawara, "Black American Cinema," 20.

8. Diawara, "Black American Cinema," 7, 19–20.

9. For a detailed discussion of the urban environment in hood films, see Paula J. Massood, *Black City Cinema: African American Urban Experiences in Film* (Philadelphia: Temple University Press, 2003).

10. variety.com.

11. Guerrero, *Framing Blackness*, 165. Guerrero makes reference to the profits that hood films made as the "second wave of blaxploitation" because the films helped boost a sluggish film industry.

12. Guerrero, *Framing Blackness*, 86. Guerrero discusses the blaxploitation formula as articulated by Thomas Cripps in *Black Film as Genre* (Bloomington: Indiana University Press, 1978), 133–134, and Gladstone Yearwood in *Black Cinema Aesthetics* (Athens: Ohio University Press, 1982), 55.

13. Diawara, "Black American Cinema," 20, 24.

14. Donald Bogle, *Toms, Coons, Mulattoes, Mammies, and Bucks: An Interpretive History of Blacks in American Films*, 3rd ed. (New York: Continuum, 1994), 347.

15. S. Craig Watkins, *Representing: Hip-Hop Culture and the Production of Black Cinema* (Chicago: University of Chicago Press, 1998), 179.

16. Nelson George, *Hip-Hop America* (New York: Penguin Books, 1999), 105.

17. Tricia Rose, *Black Noise: Rap Music and Black Culture in Contemporary America* (Hanover, N.H.: Wesleyan University Press, 1994), 5.

18. William L. Van Deburg, *Hoodlums: Black Villains and Social Bandits in American Life* (Chicago: University of Chicago Press, 2004), 182.

19. *Boyz n the Hood* was the highest grossing film in the genre earning $57.5 million, domestically. Hood films declined in popularity over the next few years. *Set It Off* (1996), a film about young women turning to crime, came the closest to *Boyz's* box office, earning $36 million. Source: variety.com.

20. Kenneth Turan, "L.A. Boyz Life: Growing Up in South Central—A Gritty *Boyz n the Hood*," *Los Angeles Times*, July 12, 1991, 1.

21. Todd Boyd, *Am I Black Enough for You? Popular Culture for the 'Hood and Beyond* (Bloomington: Indiana University Press, 1997), 83.

22. George, *Hip-Hop America*, 105.

23. Each of these films grossed over $100 million at the box office domestically. Source: variety.com.

24. Whether these images exist in a somewhat comedic context or are more grounded in the dramatic, they link masculinity not only with violence but also with a kind of hyperviolence. It is clear, however, that masculinity linked to violence differs greatly during this era with regard to race. First, in action films of the early 1990s, white male characters are significantly older than those found in hood films. Another distinction is that the films with white male characters are not meant to be taken seriously. They are essentially fantasy vehicles with major stars designed for box office appeal. In contrast, hood films are somewhat defined by their "realism." Most significant, however, is that in action-fantasy films such as *True Lies*, *The Terminator*, and so on, masculinity is defined as heroic in many cases and aberrant in others. Violent black masculinity on the other hand, until rather recently (here I'm thinking of action-fantasy films such as *Bad Boys* [1995] and *Bad Boys II* [2003] starring Will Smith and Martin Lawrence and Wesley Snipes in *Blade* [1998], *Blade 2* [2002], and *Blade: Trinity* [2004]), appears as self-hatred, as well as a representation of the whole, by virtue of less diversity in the images of black males. Finally, in terms of the audience for the films, it is also likely that the age of the characters in each genre greatly influenced the age group of the audiences.

25. This information was taken from the DVD cover for *The Education of Sonny Carson* (distributed by VCI Entertainment) and commentary by Michael Campus (director) and Sonny Carson (aka Mwalamu Imiri Abubadika). Boyz II Men made reference to *Cooley High* in the naming of their album *Cooleyhighharmony*.

26. *Cooley High* spent sixteen consecutive weeks on the "50 Top-Grossing Films" chart published weekly by *Variety*. During that time, it earned slightly over

$4 million. *Cornbread, Earl & Me* spent eight weeks on the same chart, earning nearly $1.8 million. "50 Top-Grossing Films," *Variety*, June 4–October 22, 1975.

27. Homer Hawkins and Richard Thomas, "White Policing of Black Populations: A History of Race and Social Control in America," eds. Ellis Cashmore and Eugene McLaughlin (London: Routledge, 1991), 65–86. The term has now become a part of popular culture.

28. Margo Jefferson, "Black Graffiti," *Newsweek*, July 21, 1975, 64.

29. "The Education of Sonny Carson," *Ebony*, August 1974, 157–59.

30. James P. Murray, "Lurid Movie Boom Over, but Black Films Steady On," *Variety*, January 7, 1975, 16, 74.

31. Angela Smith, "Two Fine Actors Inspire Youth in New Film," *New York Amsterdam News*, June 4, 1975, B-14.

32. For example, see Janice Radway, *Reading the Romance: Women, Patriarchy, and Popular Literature* (Chapel Hill: University of North Carolina Press, 1984). See also Henry Louis Gates Jr., "Literary Theory and the Black Tradition," in *Reception Study: From Literary Theory to Cultural Studies*, ed. James L. Machor and Philip Goldstein, 105–17 (New York: Routledge, 2001).

33. Tamar Liebes and Elihu Katz, *The Export of Meaning: Cross-Cultural Readings of* Dallas (New York: Oxford University Press, 1990). See also David Morley, *The Nationwide Audience: Structure and Decoding* (London: British Film Institute, 1980).

34. For example, see Janet Staiger, *Interpreting Films* (Princeton, N.J.: Princeton University Press, 1992); JoEllen Shively, "Cowboys and Indians: Perceptions of Western Films among American Indians and Anglos," *American Sociological Review* 57 (1992): 725–34; and Jacqueline Bobo, *Black Women as Cultural Readers* (New York: Columbia University Press, 1995).

35. For example, see Radway, *Reading the Romance*, and Bobo, *Black Women as Cultural Readers*. See also Mankekar Purnima, *Screening Culture, Viewing Politics: An Ethnography of Television, Womanhood, and Nation in Postcolonial India* (Durham, N.C.: Duke University Press, 1999).

36. For example, see Joellen Fisherkeller, "Everyday Learning about Young Adolescents in Television Culture," *Anthropology and Education Quarterly* 28, no. 4 (1997): 467–93.

37. John Leland and Donna Foote, "A Bad Omen for Black Movies," *Newsweek*, July 29, 1991, 118(5): 48–49.

38. Richard W. Stevenson, "An Anti-Gang Movie Opens to Violence." *New York Times*, July 14, 1991, sec. 1, p. 10.

39. Several books and articles have been written that situate hood films within the larger social context of American society. For example, see George, *Hip-Hop America*, and Watkins, *Representing*.

CHAPTER ONE

~

Readers and Response

Reader-Response Theory

Classic reader-response criticism, which originated in literary theory in the 1930s with Louise Rosenblatt's influential book *Literature as Exploration*,[1] examines the role of the reader in constructing the meaning of texts.[2] (Since Rosenblatt's theory stresses the transaction between the reader and the text, she does not entirely fit into the category of those classified as reader-centered approach theorists. She was included in this category, however, because she was instrumental in calling attention to the reader's role in the meaning-making process.) Reader-response critics examine the meaning of texts by questioning the reader's relationship to the text. Reader-response critics would argue that a poem cannot be understood apart from its results. Its "effects," psychological and otherwise, are essential to any accurate description of its meaning since that meaning has no effective existence outside its realization in the mind of the reader.[3]

Within this theory, several approaches have emerged whose practitioners attempt to explain the role of the reader. Generally, reader-response theorists have taken either a text-centered, reader-centered, or context-centered approach to examining the relationship between reader and text.[4]

Text-Centered Approach

According to the text-centered approach, the reader requires special training to understand the meaning of a text. In a sense, the features of the text dictate its meaning. Once the reader understands the conventions of the text, he or she will be able to make meaning. Subsequently, the process of meaning making occurs with minimal effort on the part of the reader. In this view, in short, "the reader's experience is the creation of the author."[5]

In *Mythologies*,[6] Roland Barthes examines how meaning is encoded into a text by means of ideological signs and symbols that are part of our culture. Scholars of semiotics, such as Barthes, speak of the relationship between sign, signifier, and signified. According to Barthes, the sign is an object or thing with a particular meaning. The signifier is a thing without form. The signified is the relationship between the sign and the signifier, which is the message or the myth itself—an idea. Semiologists such as Barthes argue that a sign can have only one meaning in a culture; therefore, the message can be decoded in only one way. But while ideological meaning in texts is difficult to deny, the relationship between the sign and signifier is more fluid than semiologists admit. Adherents of this theory diminish the reader's role in meaning making, and proponents of competing theories have argued that meaning making is more subjective than proponents of the text-centered approach acknowledge.

Although proponents of the text-centered approach to meaning acknowledge the role of the encoder and culture in the meaning of a text, they ignore the reader's individuality. Scholars using text-centered approaches assume for the most part that information encoded in a text is decoded in the manner in which it was intended. In most cases, they assume an "ideal reader."[7]

Reader-Centered Approach

In contrast to the text-centered approach, adherents of the reader-centered approach examine the features of readers and how their experience, knowledge, and beliefs shape the reading of a text. According to Rosenblatt, "The reader brings to the work personality traits, memories of past events, present needs and preoccupations, a particular mood of the moment, and a particular physical condition."[8] These

features may include such factors as culture, gender, and socioeconomic class. (Although Rosenblatt is not generally considered an ad-
herent of the reader-centered approach because she stresses the "transaction" between the reader and the text, her theory was instrumental
in calling attention to the reader's role in the meaning-making
process.) David Bleich argues that while "response" is individually determined and therefore subjective, "a response can acquire meaning
only in the context of a predecided community's (two or more people)
interest in knowledge."[9] In other words, a response is an initial individual reaction to a text, and knowledge is "the product of negotiation
among members of a predecided community."[10]

In "Interpreting the Variorum," Stanley Fish takes Bleich's notion
of meaning making further by introducing the idea of interpretive
communities. According to Fish, interpretive communities are groups
who share interpretive strategies for "writing" texts. He contends that
these strategies exist prior to the act of reading and therefore are used
to determine the shape of what is read.[11] In other words, interpretive
communities socially construct meanings before their participants en-
counter particular texts. This knowledge is then used to decode the
text. Individual community members decode the text according to
their own strategy and in this sense are "writing" the text. Fish contends that it is likely that one person will be a member of more than
one interpretive community and thus select among different response
strategies in engaging different texts or even the "same" text in different social contexts.

Nowhere has Fish's idea of interpretive communities been more
clearly expressed than in ethnographic research on audience responses
to the electronic media. In *The Export of Meaning: Cross-Cultural Readings of* Dallas, Tamar Liebes and Elihu Katz examined the ways in
which six ethnically diverse interpretive communities viewed the television program *Dallas*.[12] Liebes and Katz found that more "traditional
viewers" (Moroccan Jews and Arabs) viewed the program as referential or real. For instance, they talked back to the screen and related the
characters' experiences to their own lives. However, the more Western
viewers (Americans and kibbutzniks) viewed the program more criti-
cally. They tended to analyze the narrative from a more distanced perspective than did the "traditional" viewers. Liebes and Katz state that,

of the six ethnic audiences studied, the Russians were the most aware of the program's ideological "message" and attended most to the structure of the program. By contrast, the Japanese viewers (from the only culture in which the program failed) focused on the ways in which the program engages the viewer. They were concerned with the devices used to manipulate the audience. Although Liebes and Katz provided insight into how members of various cultures viewed the same television program, they did not systematically examine the difference among male and female respondents in their focus groups or attend to the impact on their results of the interactions of males and females in the same groups. As noted by Liebes and Katz, the women in some groups tended to talk less than the men, and although the investigators did not systematically examine this relationship, they suggest that some women may have been inhibited by the presence of men.

Although the scholarship on interpretive communities has been successful in identifying how responses can vary from group to group,[13] very few scholars have gone beyond noting the variations in responses of interpretive communities as wholes. None has systematically examined the process of negotiating meaning as it is articulated in interactions with socioculturally diverse others.

Another well-known theory that focuses on how readers make meaning is set forth in "Encoding/Decoding" by Stuart Hall. In this essay, Hall argues for a circular model of communication. He contends that messages are encoded into a text by the sender and are decoded by the receiver. The receiver's interpretation of the message, however, depends on his or her background, values, beliefs, and history.

Hall identifies three types of reading that can occur as a result of the encoding/decoding process: dominant, negotiated, and oppositional. Dominant or preferred readings are those interpretations that are closely aligned with the dominant ideology. In such readings, the encoded meaning equals the decoded meaning. Negotiated readings, however, rework the meanings preferred by the dominant ideology by taking into account the social differences of different responders. "Negotiating" readers understand the intent of the text as an expression of the dominant ideology, recognize their own departures from those meanings when they make them, and tend to subordinate their own personal meanings to the dominant meanings encoded by the text. Oppositional readings are made by those who may or may not understand the preferred reading but make meanings of a text in direct opposition to the dominant ideology.[14] According to scholars such as Diawara and Mayne, marginalized groups such as women and minorities often engage in oppositional reading.[15]

Critics of the encoding/decoding model, such as Lembo and Tucker and Cohen,[16] argue that Hall's theory perpetuates oppositional politics because it constructs reading processes in terms of marginalized and dominant groups. They contend that "oppositional politics is reductionistic because it ignores audiences' less rational, nonpolitically motivated, and perhaps more creative readings of texts."[17] However, in discussing the relationship between communication, culture, and meaning, Dennis Mumby argues that the process of cultural formation and deformation is at least partially a product of the power structures that characterize the relations of domination that exist between different social groups in a culture. Meaning is therefore contingent on intersubjective understanding within a community but also on the process by which certain dominant groups are able to frame the interests of competing groups within their own particular worldview. It is in this context, that ideology plays a key role in constituting the meaning formations that are built on and around the relations of domination that characterize a particular culture or institution.[18]

At least among some of its proponents, therefore, the encoding/decoding model does not assume that responses are solely politically motivated. Although Hall's encoding/decoding model can be applied to communication in general, David Bordwell discusses meaning making specifically in film.[19] In *Making Meaning: Inference and Rhetoric in the Interpretation of Cinema*, Bordwell argues that "when spectators or critics make sense of a film, the meanings they construct are of only four possible types": referential, explicit, implicit, and symptomatic. According to Bordwell, in a referential reading, the film is taken as real. For example, in *The Export of Meaning: Cross-Cultural Readings of Dallas*, Liebes and Katz found that more "traditional viewers" relate the characters' experiences to their own lives—that is, they treat it as having "real" reference to events outside the "frame" of the television drama. Alternatively (and/or simultaneously), Bordwell argues that viewers can construct explicit meanings from a film, abstracting from it a specific point or "message" that "speaks directly" to the viewer. As an example, Bordwell cites the line in *The Wizard of Oz*, "There's no place like home." Bordwell contends that implicit meanings are themes that are sometimes constructed when the viewer cannot construct a referential or explicit meaning. He argues that in this instance, the film "speaks indirectly" to the audience—that is, the viewer draws conclusions on the basis of hidden meanings in the text. Bordwell argues that if a viewer constructs either referential, explicit, or implicit meanings, he or she "assumes that the film 'knows' more or less what it is doing."[20] In contrast, symptomatic or repressed meanings are more creative. In this view, meanings are disguised in the film because the viewer believes that the film does not know what it is doing. The viewer believes that the film unconsciously exposes the artist's obsessions or the economic, political, or ideological processes in society. Bordwell cites the interpretation of *Psycho* as concealing the male fear of women's sexuality as a symptomatic meaning. He argues that symptomatic meanings are at odds with referential, explicit, and implicit meanings.

Bordwell's theory can be used to illuminate Hall's broad categories of dominant, oppositional, and negotiated readings. For instance, it is theoretically possible for a reading to be both dominant and referential or explicit. Negotiated readings can be constructed by symptomatic or implicit meanings. Oppositional readings can be produced by implicit meanings.

While the reader-centered approaches to meaning outlined here pay far more attention to the socially situated nature of meaning making than do text-centered approaches, they tend to assume that meaning is a "product," a more or less completed "result" of readers' transactions with "texts" against a backdrop of social factors that shape and constrain the reader's personal, psychological processes. An alternative would be to view meaning as an emergent process that is inherently social and interpersonally transactional—an ongoing event that occurs not only between readers and texts but also among readers as they formulate and articulate their responses to one another via different media and in different immediate social contexts. This alternative view has been suggested, if not systematically formulated or investigated, in context-centered approaches to meaning making.

Context-Centered Approach

Adherents of the context-centered approach examine the context of the reading experience in an attempt to understand how meaning is made. Janet Staiger states that "context-activated theories of reading assert that meaning is 'in' the contextual event of each reading, not 'in' one reading event rather than another."[21] By the contextual event of reading, Staiger means the totality of social and cultural affairs and texts in which a reader's engagement with texts is embedded at a particular historical moment. Thus, Staiger contends that we cannot understand how meaning is made if we examine only a single reading experience. In *Interpreting Films*, Staiger relies heavily on newspaper articles written during the time in which a film was released and to a lesser extent on personal interviews to understand the meanings attributed to a film. She contends that to achieve the most accurate picture of how meaning is made, information must be obtained from "other films produced during the same year, across cultures, races, and nations," as well as from personal interviews and newspaper articles.[22] Staiger calls this a "historical materialist" approach to interpreting film since her research involves incorporating a wide range of information obtained during a particular period. One of the main problems with the historical-materialist approach, however, is its heavy reliance on newspapers to construct (i.e., deduce) the social and informational context that viewers are assumed to bring to bear in responding to films. It is very much an open question whether filmgoers as a whole are as knowledgeable of such a "context" as newspapers might imply.

Jonathan Culler takes a more limited and institutional approach to the meaning of "context" in the interpretation of texts. He argues that there are internalized rules that govern the interpretation of a text, making reading possible. He contends that the rules for reading are communicated and shaped by the institutions that teach readers to read. By learning these conventions, the reader learns what is an "appropriate" or "acceptable" interpretation of a text. Culler refers to this as acquiring "literary competence."[23] However, this theory assumes that the reader is not confronted with conflicting institutional rules (i.e., those of school versus those of home, neighborhood, and peer group) that compete for attention. And it allows little room for divergent readings of a text. According to Culler, any reading that does not

adhere to the rules of reading codified in the dominant ideology is in-
appropriate or unacceptable.

Although the context-centered approach is useful for understanding
some of the conditions that contribute to the meanings different groups
give to texts, researchers in this tradition have tended to deduce readers' meanings from their affiliations with particular institutions at particular historical moments. In such an approach, it is easy to overlook
other factors that may play a role in shaping response.

The critical arguments in reader-response theory in general and the
context-centered approach in particular assume that the meanings people make are relatively independent of the immediate social context—
that is, the interpersonal engagements—in which they are constructed,
articulated, and negotiated. The form of communication and the context of interpersonal transactions in which people formulate and modify their responses are equally important in understanding the meaning-
making process. In this study, therefore, I analyzed meaning making as
a dynamic social process of negotiating with others—here, others who
make up a culturally diverse group of college students responding to
"hood" films both in self-moderated discussions and with one another.

In the study reported here, I applied reader-response theory and case
study methods of qualitative field research to an analysis of the responses of culturally diverse young adults to ghettocentric "street" films
to examine how the films themselves, unique characteristics that viewers bring to the films, and the immediate social context of response
shape meaning making.

My research analyzed the meaning-making responses of young adults
from various backgrounds to male-oriented, ghettocentric street films
to explore the roles of text, reader, and immediate social context in negotiating meaning-making responses to "hood" films in a culturally diverse college classroom. A "text," as defined here, is any concrete object to which people assign meaning. It includes but is not limited to
film. "Reader" refers to anyone who assigns meaning to the signs and
symbols that make up a text. For film, the "readers" are the audience
members or viewers. The "immediate social context" refers here to the
situation in which a viewer watches a film, the medium through which
the viewer responds (e.g., speech with copresent others), and the composition of the audience to whom the viewer expresses his or her re-

sponses to a text. "Meaning making" was defined here as the process through which individuals decode signs and symbols and relate them to their experience in an attempt to understand their world.[24] It is a response that one makes to a text. In this study, "meaning making" and "response" were used interchangeably.

With the consent of the Africana Studies Program at a large, urban university, students who elected to enroll in a film genre course focusing on contemporary black film—a course offered by this researcher—served as the potential participants in this study. As the normal instructional procedure of the course, all students viewed a selection of popular "street" films from the early 1990s, participated in class discussions, and wrote a response paper on a film or films (in that genre) of each student's choosing that was submitted to me (the instructor) at the end of the course. Students were informed at the first class meeting that it was my normal teaching practice (which it was) to tape-record class discussions to help me identify issues for subsequent classes but that the recorded material would not be used for other purposes without each student's specific consent.

The Films

Three ghettocentric street films were selected for the purposes of this research. A ghettocentric street film/hood film was defined here as any film that emphasized life on the street. The content is specific to urban environments. These films are overwhelmingly male oriented, often telling the story of gang members and low-level drug dealers. The genre was selected because of the controversy surrounding the impact of some of the films on their audiences when they opened in theaters across the country, a controversy with both "real-world" and theoretical significance for questions about the role of the reader, text, and immediate social context in shaping meaning.

Since I was concerned primarily with examining the interplay of the text, reader, and immediate social context in the meaning-making process and examining through descriptive qualitative analysis the differences in patterns of response, the following ghettocentric street films were chosen as the target texts: *Menace II Society* (1993), directed by Allen and Albert Hughes; *Juice* (1992), directed by Ernest Dickerson;

and *Boyz n the Hood* (1991), directed by John Singleton. These films were selected because they are representative of the genre but differ in significant ways—that is, the locales in which they were set, their representations of women and violence, and the themes of their narratives. Such differences, as well as differences in the films' aesthetic features, provided an appropriate basis for examining the extent to which and how different "texts" may evoke difference in response.

Focus Groups

Focus groups were used to elicit participants' responses to each film because of their ability to produce an environment that is conducive to generating thoughts, statements, and interactions about a particular subject matter.[25] According to Morgan, "Focus groups are useful when it comes to investigating what participants think, but they excel at uncovering why participants think as they do."[26] Such groups have been successfully used in advertising, marketing, and qualitative research studies.

In "Rethinking the Focus Group in Media and Communications Research," Lunt and Livingstone discuss the usefulness of analyzing focus groups to gain insight into public opinion formation. They contend that within this paradigm,

> identities become plural and shifting, and persuasion involves a conversation among multiple participants, challenging the notion of core social-psychological attitudes and identities. In this light, individuals are seen to continually reposition themselves in relation to the circulation of discourses.[27]

In this study, there were three focus group discussions during the course. Each was conducted immediately following the participants' viewing of one of the target films. All members of the class made up a single group. I initiated each discussion, which lasted approximately forty-five minutes, by posing a single question. Each of the three focus group discussions was audiotaped. According to Merton, audiotape is less intrusive and setup less complicated than videotape. In effect, the advantages of audiotape far outweigh the disadvantages.[28]

Throughout the discussions, there was a low level of moderator (i.e., instructor) involvement. According to Morgan, low-level involvement allows participants to express their own interests to a greater extent than when the moderator is highly involved.[29] Therefore, I did not participate in the discussions except for minimal "back-to-the-subject" prompts if the discussions moved away entirely from the films and related topics to which they gave rise.

As a former college teacher of expository writing, I used popular films and focus group discussions of them to stimulate student writing, and I have experimented with a variety of prompts to initiate the discussions. In my experience, the single question, "What is the film about?" elicited the greatest range of responses from the largest number of participants. Despite its apparent focusing of attention on the "message" of the text, the question in fact seems to be interpreted as an open invitation to address any topic related to the participants' experience of the film—their aesthetic judgments, political opinions, personal life experiences, memories of earlier viewings, comparisons with other films, and so on. Since a wide range of nondirected responses were sought in this study, my discussion-initiating prompt was the single question, "What is the film about?"

I then removed myself from the discussion, speaking only to probe a response if necessary to clarify what had been said in the group to ensure my understanding of the group's conversation (member checking) or to maintain an orderly discussion. But despite my attempt to be unobtrusive during this time, I am aware that my presence as a black female instructor for the course, only slightly older than most of the participants, in somewhat conservative dress, had some impact (if only minor) on the kind of responses given by participants.

On the last day of class, after the students' papers were returned with their grade for the course indicated, I explained to the group that I was interested in studying further their responses to *Menace II Society*, *Boyz n the Hood*, and *Juice*. At that time, I read the consent forms to the class and fielded questions. I then explained that if they chose to participate, their names would be changed and that any information they provided would be strictly confidential. It was also made clear that they were in no way obligated to participate in the study and that their participation would not impact their grade for the course, which they would already have received. Finally, I instructed the class that any student who agreed to allow his or her responses to be used in the study should return the consent form and the background questionnaire in a sealed envelope to me. The questionnaire solicited information about ethnicity, education, family income, and other factors.[30] Once the signed student consent forms and background questionnaires were returned, the oral responses of the participant were used in the study.

The Social Audience

In "Women's Genres," Annette Kuhn draws a distinction between media viewers as members of a "social audience" and as "spectators." According to Kuhn, a social audience is made up of actual viewers, or people who actively seek out a particular film or television program. Spectators are people who have been brought together by a researcher for the purpose of analyzing the meaning-making process. Kuhn argues that "spectator" research does not provide a realistic view of interpretation and society because it does not describe people who are targeted by or attracted to a particular genre. In real life, only the people exposed by their own choice to a film or television program will be directly affected by it.[31] While most studies use homogeneous groups of people brought together specifically for a research project, Bobo and Radway examined groups that were formed on the basis of their self-evidenced interest in the subject matter.[32]

According to Kuhn's definitions, the participants in this study may be characterized as members of a social audience in that they elected to enroll in the course because of a particular interest in black cinema. Therefore, their responses to the films were more relevant to the responses of larger, self-selected audiences for the films than the responses of a group constructed purely for the purposes of studying meaning making.

Participants

Since the immediate social context (i.e., composition of the group) is central to the idea that the dynamics of group response has a significant impact on how meaning is made, it is important to address how participants were selected. Fourteen students who enrolled in an elective film genre course (specifically on African American films) at a major university were asked to participate in the study. The course provides a sociohistorical look at films directed by black American filmmakers since the 1970s—starting with the blaxploitation era and ending with the current films under study, hood films. There was a main text for the course and several articles.[33] I served as the instructor for the class.

Since the participants were self-selected, it was not possible to predict with any precision the ethnic, gender, or socioeconomic characteristics of group members, although a survey of similar courses indicated that they draw a diverse population of males and females, African and European Americans, Asians and Asian Americans, and young people from both middle- and lower-socioeconomic backgrounds. At the end of the course, after the students had been informed of their grades, volunteers were asked to complete a background questionnaire on their ethnic self-identification and socioeconomic status. Only those who returned the questionnaire were profiled in the results of the study on the basis of the answers they provide. All fourteen students completed the questionnaire. Pseudonyms have been used for the participants throughout this report.

Participants in the study ranged in age from nineteen to twenty-nine years old. The mean age for the group was 21.9 years. With respect to ethnicity, seven major categories were constructed from the students' responses: African American, European American, Asian American, Asian, Hispanic, ethnically/racially mixed black, and ethnically/racially mixed nonblack.[34] (Because of the focus on the image of African Americans in the films under study, any participant who indicated a mixed racial or ethnic heritage was grouped according to whether he or she categorized him- or herself as at least in part black.) In sum, there were four European American participants (two males and two females), four African American females, one Latina, two mixed-black participants (one male and one female), one ethnically mixed-nonblack male, one Asian American female, and one Asian female.

With the exception of four students (Mary, Cathy, Mark, and Soo), all participants grew up on the East Coast of the United States. Six of the students were raised in the New York City area (Brenda, David,

Greg, Paula, Donna, and Robert). And all the participants met the requirements for middle-class membership.[35]

On the first day of class, it became apparent who would be most active for the next six weeks. The small room had a long conference table in it. Comfortably, it could seat ten people. The remaining students would have to sit in chairs that lined the walls. This configuration made it difficult for anyone to hide in the room. There was a large-screen television set near the door. As participants entered the space for the first time, some seemed surprised that I was seated at the head of the table with my roster out to check names. As they assumed their seats, in which most would remain for the course of the semester, it became clear that there were some very distinct personalities.

Next I describe the responses given in the background questionnaire by select participants. They are five of the most active participants described in this study. Here they are used to illustrate and detail the composition of the group.

Donna

In the background questionnaire, Donna identified herself as a twenty-nine-year-old black female in her junior year of college. She was single and had not lived with a parent or guardian for the past five years. Donna had worked full-time for less than twelve months in a job for which she earned more than $36,000 a year. She had never served a prison term or been an unwed teenage parent. Although Donna was raised in California, at the time of the study she was living in New Jersey. Based on the information Donna provided in the background questionnaire, she met the criteria for middle-class membership.

On the first day of class, Donna wore blue spandex bike shorts and carried rollerblades. She was a light-brown-skinned woman with strawberry blond dreadlocks. On meeting her, I quickly formed the impression that she was her own person. Donna's clothing reflected her boldness, as did the confidence with which she spoke. Initially, she appeared cautious, if not outright suspicious, of her new surroundings. Donna's suspicion was reflected in the assertive manner in which she asked me questions about myself and the requirements for the course and in her general aloofness toward members of the group. As time went on, however, her demeanor softened, and she became friendlier.

Brenda

In the background questionnaire, Brenda identified herself as a nineteen-year-old African American female. She was a junior in college who had permanently lived with a parent or guardian during the past five years. There were a total of three people living in her home, including a divorced head of household who had attended college and who had held a full-time position for the past five years, with a total gross household income of over $36,000 a year. No one in the home had served a prison term or been a unwed teenage parent. Brenda was raised and, at the time of the study, still lived in Harlem. Based on the previously mentioned responses, Brenda was categorized as middle class.

When I first met Brenda, she took a seat at the head of the table opposite me. She maintained that position throughout the semester. Brenda was thoughtful and soft spoken. Her manner and relative position at the table led me to believe that she was a confident young lady. She had medium brown skin and short black hair.

Erika

In the background questionnaire, Erika identified herself as a twenty-two-year-old senior of black and Filipino heritage. Within the past five years, she had lived with both of her parents. Their gross monthly income was over $3,000. The head of household had a college degree and had worked for the past five years. At the time of the study, there were a total of five people in the home. No one in the household had served a prison term or been an unwed teenage parent. Based on the aforementioned responses, Erika was categorized as middle class.

Erika was a brown-skinned woman with shoulder-length silky black hair. From the first day I met her, she seemed friendly and at ease. Erika often conversed with the other members of the group before class.

Tracie

In the background questionnaire, Tracie identified herself as a twenty-year-old woman of Caucasian/Jewish descent. She was a senior in college who had lived with her parents within the past five years. At the time of the study, there were four people living in the home. The head of household had attended graduate school and held a full-time job for the past five years. The family's total gross monthly income was over

$3,000. No one in the household had ever served a prison term or been an unwed teenage parent. Based on the previously mentioned responses, Tracie was categorized as middle class.

Tracie, who had long black curly hair, often sat in the shadows of other students. Even from my vantage point at the head of the table, she always seemed to be blocked by someone else. Throughout the course, she sat in the same location, next to the same person (Samantha). She seemed shy and somewhat uncomfortable in that her voice sometimes shook when she spoke. I do not think that I ever saw her smile, even when someone told a joke.

Mark

Mark (who left his age blank in the questionnaire) was a senior who characterized himself as black, white, and Native American. Within the past five years, he had lived with a parent or guardian who was divorced. At the time of the study, there were four people in the home. The head of household had attended graduate school and had worked full-time for the past five years, earning a gross monthly income of over $3,000. No one in the household had served a prison term or been an unwed teenage parent. Based on the information that Mark provided in the background questionnaire, he met the requirements for middle-class membership.

Mark had fair skin and dark curly hair. From the first day I met him, he was friendly and outspoken—constantly asking questions and offering his insights into comments made by other students. Mark maintained this demeanor throughout the course of the semester. On one occasion, he provided me with additional information about his background when he asked me if he could turn in his paper early because he was going out of town. When I inquired where he was going, he told me that he was participating in a Native American religious ceremony in New Mexico. On another occasion, he mentioned to the members of the class that he was adopted.

Analysis

Students screened the films in a university classroom, during class, as part of the normal conduct of the course. The participants' viewing of the films in a group setting was appropriate because the moviegoing experience among adolescents and young adults tends to be a group event. As participants viewed the films, field notes were taken to note their reactions (laughter, talking, and so on) to specific images. For the most part, however, students remained silent while screening the films.

Each focus group discussion was audiotaped, and the tapes were transcribed verbatim. In addition, I took field notes during the discussion, particularly attending to nonverbal behavior and the tone of statements and exchanges. When the discussions were over, all participants were asked to write a response paper. For each focus group discussion, I examined such dynamics as extent and distribution of participation, points of conflict, means of conflict management and resolution, and establishing or changing of the topic. Then I examined the themes and metathemes that emerged from the data as they related to the content of the films themselves. For the purpose of this study, themes were inferences made by linking the ideas under the various topics or categories together, which initially organized the data.

After examining the group discussion as a whole for each film, I focused on those of the participants who consented to have their engagement reported (anonymously) and who were most active in the discussions for a more detailed analysis of how meanings were constructed and negotiated socially by individual participants. The following questions were developed in part from my readings in reader-response literature and my experience as a teacher but, most important, from my reading and re-reading of the transcripts for each discussion and the response papers.

One of the most important aspects of my analysis was where participants focused their attention. In other words, what were the primary themes discussed by participants? What themes did the participant's talk focus on? Did the participant's talk focus on the characteristics of the film itself? On the participant's own personal experience? Or on the social/political world outside the film?

I also examined the critical orientation of each participant, that is, the relative position or role that the participant assumed in responding to the film. For instance, how did the participant articulate his or her position? What area(s) of knowledge—for example, psychological, sociological, aesthetic, self, or political—were brought to bear?

A participant's aesthetic distance to the text was also important in analyzing the responses to a genre that elicited so much social concern and debate. Edward Bullough's essay "'Psychical Distance' as a Factor in Art and an Aesthetic Principle" was significant in shaping current theories of audience response because it drew attention to the reader's emotional relationship to a text.[36] Scholars building on Bullough's theory have argued that the viewer's aesthetic distance is related to his or her ability to identify with the characters. In a sense, it is the degree to which the viewer links the features of the text to human characteristics.[37] It is the participant's emotional connection to the film. For example, what was the emotional tone of the participant's talk? In this study, the tone of a response (or responses) is categorized as either "cool," "warm," or "hot." A cool response is one in which participants do not appear to be very emotionally connected to the text. Their talk is relatively of a low intensity. A warm response suggests that participants are more or less engaged when talking about the text. The talk is of moderate intensity. Responses are categorized as hot if participants engaged in high-intensity talk during the discussion. As such, they were extremely emotional when talking about the text.

In my analysis, I also looked at conflict management and resolution—the means by which the participant addressed and negotiated differences of opinion. For instance, how did the participant deal with controversial issues? With challenges to his or her statements? Did the participant deny, condition, modify, intensify, or accept his or her statements in the face of actual or anticipated rebuttals?

Notes

1. Louise Rosenblatt, *Literature as Exploration* (New York: D. Appleton-Century, 1938).

2. Jane Tompkins, ed., *Reader-Response Criticism* (Baltimore: The Johns Hopkins University Press, 1980), ix–x.

3. Tompkins, *Reader-Response Criticism*, ix.

4. Janet Staiger, *Interpreting Films* (Princeton, N.J.: Princeton University Press, 1992).

5. Tompkins, *Reader-Response Criticism*, xvii.

6. Roland Barthes, *Mythologies* (New York: Hill and Wang, 1972).

7. Gerald Prince, "Introduction to the Study of the Narratee," In *Reader-Response Criticism*, ed. Jane P. Tompkins (Baltimore: The Johns Hopkins University Press, 1980), 9.

8. Rosenblatt, *Literature as Exploration*, 37.

9. David Bleich, "Epistemological Assumptions in the Study of Response," in Tompkins, *Reader-Response Criticism*, 158.

10. Tompkins, *Reader-Response Criticism*, xx–xxi.

11. Stanley Fish, "Interpreting the Variorum," in Tompkins, *Reader-Response Criticism*, 182.

12. Tamar Liebes and Elihu Katz, *The Export of Meaning: Cross-Cultural Readings of Dallas* (New York: Oxford University Press, 1990).

13. JoEllen Shively, "Cowboys and Indians: Perceptions of Western Films among American Indians and Anglos," *American Sociological Review* 57 (1992): 725–34. See also David Morley, *The Nationwide Audience: Structure and Decoding* (London: British Film Institute, 1980).

14. Stuart Hall, "Encoding/Decoding," in *Culture, Media, Language*, ed. Stuart Hall, Dorothy Hobson, Andrew Lowe, and Paul Willis (London: Hutchinson, 1980), 128–38.

15. Manthia Diawara, "Black American Cinema: The New Realism," in *Black American Cinema*, ed. Manthia Diawara (New York: Routledge, 1993), 3–25. See also Judith Mayne, *Cinema and Spectatorship* (New York: Routledge, 1993).

16. Ron Lembo and Kathy Tucker, "Culture, Television, and Opposition: Rethinking Cultural Studies," *Critical Studies in Mass Communication* 7 (1990): 97–116; Jeff Cohen, "The 'Relevance' of Cultural Identity in Audiences' Interpretations of Mass Media," *Critical Studies in Mass Communication* 8 (1991): 442–54.

17. Cohen, "The 'Relevance' of Cultural Identity in Audiences' Interpretations of Mass Media," 111.

18. Dennis Mumby, "Ideology and the Social Construction of Meaning: A Communication Perspective," *Communication Quarterly* 37 (1989): 293.

19. David Bordwell, *Making Meaning: Inference and Rhetoric in the Interpretation of Cinema* (Cambridge, Mass.: Harvard University Press, 1989).

20. David Bordwell, *Making Meaning*, 8–9.

21. Staiger, *Interpreting Films*, 47.

22. Staiger, *Interpreting Films*, 97.

23. Jonathan Culler, "Literary Competence," in Tompkins, *Reader-Response Criticism*, 108, 111–15.

24. Hall, "Encoding/Decoding."

25. Robert Merton, Marjorie Fiske, and Patricia L. Kendall, *Focused Interview: A Manual of Problems and Procedures*, 2nd ed. (New York: Free Press, 1990).

26. David Morgan, *Focus Groups as Qualitative Research* (Newbury Park, Calif.: Sage Publications, 1988), 25.

27. Peter Lunt and Sonia Livingstone, "Rethinking Focus Groups in Media and Communications Research," *Journal of Communication* 46, no. 2 (1996): 88.

28. Merton et al., *Focused Interview*, 62.

29. Morgan, *Focus Groups as Qualitative Research*, 50.

30. See appendix C. The questionnaire was based in part on Janice Radway's *Reading the Romance: Women, Patriarchy, and Popular Culture* (Chapel Hill: University of North Carolina Press, 1984), and JoEllen Shively, "Cowboys and Indians: The Perception of Western Films among American Indians and Anglo Americans," Ph.D. diss., Stanford University, 1990.

31. Annette Kuhn, "Women's Genres: Annette Kuhn Considers Melodrama, Soap Opera and Theory," *Screen* 25, no. 1 (1984): 18–28.

32. Morley, *The Nationwide Audience*; Shively, "Cowboys and Indians"; Liebes and Katz, *The Export of Meaning*. For studies that examine viewers who are brought together by their interest in the subject, see Jacqueline Bobo, *Black Women as Cultural Readers* (New York: Columbia University Press, 1995), and Radway, *Reading the Romance*.

33. The main text used for the course was *Framing Blackness: The African American Image in Film* by Ed Guerrero. Several articles related to the critical analysis of specific films were also used. During the semester, students viewed the following films: *Black Shadows on a Silver Screen* (1986), *Menace II Society* (1993), *Sweet Sweetback's Baadasssss Song* (1971), *Shaft* (1971), *Superfly* (1972), *Daughters of the Dust* (1991), *She's Gotta Have It* (1986), *To Sleep with Anger* (1990), *Juice* (1992), and *Boyz n the Hood* (1991). The films were not always viewed in chronological order. Scheduling conflicts that limited their availability are not unusual occurrences during a semester. Other changes were made to highlight particular themes. Because the study took place during a six-week summer session, the films were viewed fairly close together. The order in which the hood films were shown was considered of only minor significance given that the vast majority (and most active) of participants had already seen at least two of the films more than one time and, as such, had participated to some extent in the interpretive process. (For a brief synopsis of the films on the syllabus and the general responses of participants to other films during the course of the semester, see appendices A and B.) If participants discussed other films on the syllabus during their discussion of hood films (which they did not),

it would have been included in this study. And, while the specific impact of hood films on other films on the syllabus is intriguing, it is beyond the scope of this research. What was most important is how the viewer does or does not articulate his or her viewing experiences among culturally diverse others (i.e., the composition of the audience) when discussing hood films. The main purpose of the study is to explore how meaning is constructed as it is expressed to specific others in dialogue and how the dynamics of the dialogue and the relations among the participants shape the meanings they give to texts.

34. Participants were asked an open-ended question to ascertain their ethnic and/or racial identity. Because of the wide variety of responses, their answers were collapsed into larger categories. For example, if a student wrote that he is English/Irish/Afghanistan, for the purposes of this study he was categorized as ethnically mixed nonblack. Additional information was teased out if it became relevant during the group discussions. But generally, students defined themselves in the classroom setting in very broad terms (i.e., black or white). While all these categories are somewhat problematic, as constructions of race typically are, they serve one of the purposes of this study, namely, to highlight the responses of those who consider themselves at least part black and how they respond in a multicultural setting.

35. Participants were grouped according to socioeconomic class on the basis of the answers they provided in the background questionnaire. A participant would have been categorized as socioeconomically "lower class" if his or her reported family income was below the poverty threshold (based on the U.S. Bureau of the Census (1996) table "Poverty Thresholds in 1996, by Size of Family and Number of Related Children under 18 Years") and/or he or she met at least two of the following criteria: 1) family was dependent on public assistance, 2) parents were chronically unemployed, 3) a family member had been convicted of a violent crime, and 4) a family member was a teenage single parent. "Middle-class" participants were defined as students whose family income exceeded the poverty level and 1) whose families did not include single teenage parents, 2) whose families did not include any member who had been convicted of a violent crime, and 3) whose parent(s) were regularly employed. The educational level of his or her parent(s) also played a role in determining class membership. For a discussion of the criteria on which participants were defined as middle or lower class and the basis for the questions on the background questionnaire, see "Challenge to Affluence—The Emergence of an 'Under-Class'" by Gunnar Myrdal (part of a section titled "Objective Dimensions of Inequality") in Celia S. Heller, ed., *Structured Social Inequality: A Reader in Comparative Social Stratification* (New York: Macmillan Publishing, 1987). *See also* page 20, note 29.

36. Edward Bullough, "'Psychical Distance' as a Factor in Art and an Aesthetic Principle." *British Journal of Psychology* 5 (1912): 87–118.

37. Andre Bazin, *What Is Cinema?*, trans. Hugh Gray, 2 vols. (Berkeley: University of California Press, 1967–1971); Daphna Ben Chaim, *Distance in the Theatre: The Aesthetics of Audience Response* (Ann Arbor, Mich.: UMI Research, 1984).

CHAPTER TWO

~

"America's Worst Nightmare": Reading *Menace II Society*

Kids come in and see the violent scenes and they take [*Menace II Society*] to be like other movies. They cheer at the beginning. Laugh. But, by the end, it just comes up and knocks them over the head, 'cause they never expect those characters were going to get mowed down in the third act. . . . You bring them in, you appall them, you make them sick from the violence.

—Albert Hughes[1]

The first film participants viewed in the hood genre was *Menace II Society* (1993) directed by Allen and Albert Hughes. The Hughes brothers conceived the story with Tyger Williams, who also wrote the screenplay. It was the first film in the hood genre watched by participants. The film, according to its directors, "is the story of how a boy becomes a gangster." Set in South-Central Los Angeles, it examines the life of Caine (Tyrin Turner) and the violent world he inhabits. Aside from its narrative, *Menace II Society* can be further distinguished from other films in the genre by its use of voice-over narration, historical black-and-white footage, and stylized violence.

The Narrative

In the opening scene of the film, O-Dog (Larenz Tate) and Caine are in a convenience store. After a few verbal exchanges with the Korean shop owner, O-Dog shoots and kills him after he makes a comment about his mother. Shocked, Caine drops the beer he is drinking on the ground. As an afterthought, O-Dog robs the convenience store. Before the pair escape, O-Dog grabs the surveillance tape, which has recorded the murder and the robbery. He then shoots and kills the shopkeeper's wife.

The scene then shifts to black-and-white footage of the 1965 race riots in Watts, California. Caine, who narrates the tale, comments that after the riots, the drugs started. The scene then switches to a party at Caine's childhood home, where Caine explains (in narration) that his father (Samuel L. Jackson) sells dope and that his mother (Khandi Alexander) is a heroin addict. During the party, Caine sees his father shoot to death a man who owes him money. Also at the party is Pernell (Glenn Plummer), a local hustler who takes Caine under his wing and teaches him about life on the streets.

Forward to present day. Caine is a dope dealer about to graduate from high school. Since Pernell is serving a life sentence in prison, Caine feels obligated to look after Pernell's girlfriend Ronnie (Jada Pinkett) and their son Anthony (Jullian Roy Doster). Through voice-over, Caine explains that he went to live with his grandparents (Marilyn Coleman and Arnold Johnson) when he was ten because his father had been killed in a drug deal and his mother died of a drug overdose.

At a party after Caine's graduation from high school, O-Dog brags about the convenience store robbery—showing the videotape over and over to his friends. During the party, Caine and his friends decide to get something to eat. En route, Caine is involved in a carjacking in which he is shot and his cousin Harold killed. O-Dog then convinces him to get revenge on the boys who killed Harold. After shooting the perpetrators to death at a drive-through window, Caine explains (in narration) that he does not feel any better, nor does he feel remorse.

Some time later, O-Dog and Caine are caught in a parking garage trying to steal a car. At the police station, O-Dog is being released from custody because he is a minor without a record. Caine, on the other hand, is interrogated by a police detective about the convenience store robbery. His fingerprints have been found on the broken beer bottle. Caine is later released for lack of evidence. After that incident, two of Caine's friends, Sharif (Vonte Sweet) and Stacy (Ryan Williams), try to convince him to move to Kansas with them so that he can have a better life.

When Sharif visits his father, Mr. Butler (Charles S. Dutton), at the school where he teaches, Mr. Butler teases Sharif about his trip to Kansas. "You're going to go up there, mess around and bring one of your devils to my house." He then laughs as he tells Sharif that he knows he's been "checkin' out them white girls." Sharif tells his father that he knows how he feels about his black women. Shortly thereafter, Caine walks in. Mr. Butler then asks Caine what he plans to do with his life. He tells Caine that Sharif used to get into all kinds of trouble until he found The Nation.[2] He tells Caine to make whatever changes he has to make in order to survive. Driving home, Caine and Sharif are beaten up by the police and dropped off on the wrong side of town—a Latino neighborhood. In narration, Caine explains that the cops thought that the Latino gangs would finish them off, but instead they took him and Sharif to the hospital. When Ronnie visits Caine in the hospital, she tries to convince him to move with her to Atlanta so that he can begin a new life with her and Anthony. Caine tells her that he will think about it.

At Ronnie's going-away party, Caine loses his temper when Chauncy (Clifton Powell), an old acquaintance, makes a pass at her. Caine then pistol-whips Chauncy until O-Dog breaks it up. Later that night, Caine gets a phone call from Ilena (Erin Leshawn Wiley), a woman he met at a barbecue, who tells him that she is pregnant with his child. Caine tells Ilena that the baby is not his and that he does not have time for her.

The next day, Chauncy, in an act of revenge, mails the videotape of the murders in the convenience store to the police. When Ronnie and Caine visit Pernell in prison, Pernell tells Caine to go to Atlanta with Ronnie. Pernell also tells him to teach his son that the way they grew up was wrong. At that moment, Caine decides to move to Atlanta. Meanwhile, Ilena has told her cousin about the pregnancy. Soon after, he confronts Caine on his grandparents' lawn. After Caine nearly stomps Ilena's cousin to death, his grandparents ask him to leave their home because they can no longer help him.

On the day that Ronnie plans to move to Atlanta, Caine finds out that the police are looking for him and O-Dog. As they load boxes onto the van, Sharif and Caine are killed in a drive-by shooting, perpetrated by Ilena's cousin and his gang. As Caine's life literally passes before his eyes, the action cuts to O-Dog as he is being placed into a police car. In voice-over, Caine states, "It all catches up with you in the end." In retrospect, he had done too much in his life to go back.

Culturally Diverse Readers

To explore the role of immediate social context in meaning making, I tape-recorded and analyzed the group discussions of college undergraduates of diverse cultural backgrounds. Participants responded to the film *Menace II Society* in a classroom setting at a major research university. *Menace* was selected because it was the site of violent activity at the time of its theatrical release. Twelve students were present on the day of the discussion, ten women and two men. At the end of the semester, students completed a background questionnaire in which they self-identified their race/ethnicity. Of the two men in the group, one identified himself as Irish, Italian, and Afghani (Robert) and the other of mixed racial heritage, which included black, Native American, and white (Mark). Of the ten women in the class, there was one Latina (Samantha), one Caucasian (Cathy), and one Jewish/Caucasian (Tracie). One student identified herself as Asian (Soo) and another as Asian American (Mary). There were three women in the class who identified themselves as African American (Paula, Donna, and Brenda) and another woman who considered herself both black and Filipino (Erika). In answering a series of questions regarding household income, educational level of parents, and so on, all students indicated a middle-class background.

Immediately after viewing the film, students were asked to express their opinions about what they had seen. I started the discussion by asking them to tell me what the film was about. From that point on, my participation in the group was minimal—designed only to keep the conversation going. As a result, the direction of the conversation was always shaped by a member of the group. Since *Menace II Society* was the first film the participants screened in class, I was somewhat concerned that they would not feel comfortable enough to express themselves and to initiate new topics for discussion. However, that was not the case. To my surprise, the conversation flowed rather freely. In order to identify the students who played a role in shaping the discussion and therefore held some degree of power within the group, I looked at who established or changed topics. I also looked at the types of topics raised and how often in order to determine what topics were of greatest importance to the group.

The Discussion

Donna, an African American female some eight or nine years older than most of the group, was the first person to respond to my initial question. She stated, "It [*Menace II Society*] wanted to try and let people know that there is a way. . . . You can get out of the situation and decide that you want to live." However, she quickly began to talk about the "intended message" of the film in relationship to the "actual message" received by audience members, unlike herself. Donna argued that the film was "not positive" because it "glamorized drugs" and "glorified violence" and would therefore not be interpreted positively by its target audience—inner-city youth. (Later in the discussion, she revealed that her analysis was based on her personal contact with the kind of people represented in the film.) From her lengthy talk on the subject, she appeared to be more interested in discussing the reactions of others to the film rather than her own. After she spoke, the room was silent, which would seem to indicate the group's apprehension about the topic. (From an analysis of subsequent dialogue, it appeared that, initially, participants were quite unfamiliar with one another and unsure about how others would respond to their ideas.) So I asked them whether they agreed or disagreed with her statement.

Brenda, an African American woman, stated that she agreed with Donna about the reaction of some black viewers, particularly inner-city teenagers. She added that the film might present a glorified image to the "uneducated viewer." "I think that an audience like the characters depicted would see a glorified image of the killing or the drugs. But to

a more educated audience you get the interpretation that Donna got."
Mary, an Asian American woman, then brought the discussion back to
the "message" of the film in an attempt to show that the film did not
glorify violence. In response, Tracie, who identified herself as Caucasian and Jewish, returned the conversation to the audience and introduced into the discussion the topic of the film's "realism" as it related to her own personal experience. "I might not live in it, but I am
aware. Just like I'm aware of people killing each other—regardless of
who's killing who." The conversation continued to bounce back and
forth on the three topics initially raised—the audience's response to the
film, the film's "realism," and the film's "message." Then Donna introduced the role of the director into the discussion as additional support
for her argument concerning the film's exaggerated representation of a
ghetto environment:

> I've been in projects from California to the East Coast and I have yet to
> see. . . . Whenever they [the directors] showed where Caine lived with
> his grandparents . . . I mean, every fifty feet you saw somebody standing
> out there drinking, standing around smoking pot. You know for people
> here who have never been . . . and everyone's watching the realism . . .
> to me that wasn't very realistic.

The debate on that topic continued as participants relied on their
personal exposure to the environment represented in the film and the
film's aesthetic structure (e.g., the behavior of characters represented
in that environment) to support their statements. Tracie then introduced other films into the conversation in order to support her view
that the directors had the right to represent the environment the way
they saw it. She argued that it was up to the audience to interpret the
film. The conversation then returned to the film's target audience—
inner-city teenagers.

The topics of the discussion continued to shift between the "message" and the responsibility of the director until Robert, an ethnically
mixed (nonblack) male, introduced a more personal note into the conversation by discussing how he viewed the characters in the film and
the conditions under which they lived:

> From my point of view, I just thought that the government threw drugs in to calm them [the residents of the ghetto] down. Drugs just don't hit after riots. Something's wrong. These kids grew up in there. They're not bad. It's not their fault. They're surviving.

However, in the next statement, Paula, an African American woman, returned the conversation to an explanation of why others interpreted the films differently—attributing a possible "misinterpretation" of the film to the age of audience members.

Samantha, the only Latina in the class, responded to that comment but returned to the topic of the responsibility of the director, citing the representation of Latinos in the film. Samantha appeared to raise the issue in an attempt to gain acknowledgment from the group that the directors represented Hispanics in a "responsible" or positive manner. However, without commenting on the representation of Latinos in the film, Tracie began to discuss the representation of white women in the film and quickly moved into her own personal experience with interracial dating. Later, she returned to the "message" of the film and the audience's interpretation of it. After incorporating Tracie's personal comments about the audience, Brenda attempted to explain the statement made in the film by Mr. Butler about black men dating white women ("bringing a devil home"). However, it seemed that Erika took her comment as a personal attack on black women. She stated, "As a black woman, I take offense that you say black women haven't reached the knowledge that white women have." From her comment, it appeared that Brenda's perceived negative comment about black women created a tension that shaped the way that future statements were interpreted by some members of the group. From there, the conversation evolved into a sociological discussion of why black men date white women. During the course of the debate, Mark's attempt to bring the conversation back to the film failed, as Erika returned to the discussion on interracial dating. The discussion finally ended when Brenda stated that she agreed with the women, although she was having trouble verbalizing what she meant. Donna then reintroduced the discussion of the director's responsibility to his audience, which continued until time ran out.

Establishing and Changing Topics

Overall, there were sixteen major shifts in the focus of the conversation precipitated by nine of the twelve participants present that day. Eight major topics were discussed among group members: the film's "message," or moral of the film; generalizations about the response of other viewers or the "audience" for the film; the representation of criminal activity in the film, as reflected in their character analysis of O-Dog and Caine; the degree to which the film was "realistic"; their experiential connection to the film, that is, their personal experience in either watching the film or knowing the kind of environment represented in the film; the responsibility or role of the director to his audience; the representation of nonblacks or "others" in the film; and the reasons for black men or women dating white men or women (and vice versa) in our society, that is, the representation of interracial dating in the film.

The majority of the topics raised during the discussion (audience, experiential connection, interracial dating, realism, and role of director) were categorized as "outside the world of the film" in that they were only indirectly related to the specifics of the text. Generally, this seemed to suggest that Menace was used by the participants to address societal concerns—issues that transcended the film itself.

Further, many of the topics raised seemed to resurface at other times throughout the discussion. Participants, however, seemed most concerned with the audience for the film, as the topic resurfaced on eight occasions and was prevalent throughout much of the conversation. They also seemed to frequently return to a discussion of what they perceived to be the film's "message" and the role of the director—which seemed to be an indication of the connection they established between the effect of the "message," the audience's interpretation of that "message," and the director's artistic license in presenting a black American, ghetto environment. Overall, participants seemed to take into account the responses of the other members of the group, as they addressed the old topic before introducing a new one. This seemed to suggest that participants consistently thought about the issues that caught their attention during the circulation of other ideas.

Although twelve students were present on the day of the screening and discussion, the conversation was controlled primarily by four women: Erika, Donna, Tracie, and Brenda. Of the participants who changed the topic on more than one occasion, Donna appeared to be the most determined to shape the conversation into what was important to her—the response of the audience to the film. From the beginning, she articulated her views. When I asked participants to tell me what the film was about, Donna was the first person to speak. This appeared to be an indication of her strong interest in the subject. The other women who played a significant role in shaping the discussion identified themselves as at least in part black (with the exception of Tracie, who indicated that she is both Caucasian and Jewish). Two of the students, Soo (an Asian American student) and Cathy (a European American student), did not speak at all, and the remaining six students present spoke only briefly. All the students present who considered themselves at least in part black or African American (six) contributed to the discussion. Of the three participants who claimed European or a racially/ethnically mixed (nonblack) background, two participated in the discussion. Of the two participants who claimed an Asian heritage, only one spoke. Since all appeared to listen attentively, by making eye contact with each speaker, the silence of those who did not speak was not attributed to a lack of interest since participants were part of a self-selected group who voluntarily enrolled in a course on black cinema.

Clearly, the women of African descent controlled the flow of the discussion, with talk that focused on the world outside the film. Thus, they seemed to hold the power within the group. While the gender and ethnic/racial makeup of the class influenced the topics under discussion, the discussion also seemed to be greatly influenced by Donna, whose primary concern seemed to be teaching nonpresent and present "others" what ghetto life is really about. Overall, Donna's remarks were more political than the rest of the group, who generally discussed the topics raised from a sociological perspective.

Points of Conflict: The Representation of Others

Generally, participants in the group were cordial in expressing their opinions about the film until their discussion of the representation of others. After discussing the audience's response to the film, Samantha (the only Hispanic member in the group) talked specifically about the "Latin issue" in the film. She commented that you rarely see Latins portrayed "responsibly" in film. In essence, Samantha seemed to say that it was good to see positive images of Latinos in film. She explained that although they (the group) were talking about the reaction of blacks and whites to *Menace*, "it is important to look at the relationship between blacks and Latinos in the film." In effect, she was stating that Latinos should be included in the discussion because they were also affected by the representation of themselves in ghettocentric film. Significantly, no one in the class responded directly to her comment. This lack of response appeared to be the type of apathy to which Samantha was referring, concerning issues that did not present themselves in "black and white"—reflecting much of the discussion on race relations in American society. The "nonresponse" of group members seemed to be an acknowledgment of her opinion because the subject matter was not directly relevant to the interests of the largely non-Hispanic group. In effect, the topic died out because Samantha did not find support for her argument. While it was possible that the members of the group considered her concerns valid, it seemed as though they did not find them relevant to their experience at that particular point in time.

Nevertheless, Samantha's comment appeared to serve as catalyst for Tracie to voice her opinion about the representation of white women in the film. It was her comment that sparked a long debate that moved the conversation from the film into a discussion on interracial dating:

> I notice when Mr. Butler was talking to Sharif [he said that] bringing home a white woman would be bringing home the devil. My boyfriend is black and I took personal offense to that. . . . But that exists out there. . . . My boyfriend's not Jewish and I'm Jewish. That's a big problem with my family. But it goes both ways.

Clearly, Tracie's interpretation of the scene was tinged by her experience as a white woman dating a black man. It appeared that because of her close connection to the subject, she could not separate the film from her own reality. The film, therefore, forced Tracie to confront her own sense of "whiteness" in relation to a film in which she was characterized as "other." In response to Tracie's statement, Brenda, who attempted to bring the conversation back to the film by explaining what

Mr. Butler meant, caused some concern and confusion among the black women of African descent in the class:

> I understand the devil part offending you in every way. Completely. I sympathize with you about that. But I think more that his point was, so many black men get educated and find Allah and you know, educate themselves. And black women haven't. . . . All black women haven't reached that pinnacle of knowledge yet. And they turn to the white woman because you have—almost.

After Brenda acknowledged Tracie's feelings, she tried to bring the conversation back to an analysis of the scene. However, Tracie seemed to have sensed that the group was disturbed by Brenda's remark in that she nodded in approval after Brenda's comment but seemed to retreat from the discussion in an attempt to avoid a confrontation. The following dialogue by Erika was taken from the conversation that took place in response to Brenda's statement:

> *Erika*: As a black woman, I take offense that you say black women haven't reached the knowledge that white women have.

The response to Brenda's statement shifted the focus of the conversation from white women to black women. In clearly defining herself as a black woman, Erika seemed to want Brenda to know that she had the right to be upset by her remarks. Erika had chosen to identify squarely with black women, although in her background questionnaire she stated that she was both Filipino and black. It appeared that as the conversation became more personal, it heated up, causing Erika to assert that part of her identity was offended. The conversation continued as Brenda tried to defend herself:

> *Brenda*: Not all black women. What I'm saying is that, a lot of times before black men decide they want to take their chances with another black woman that might know . . .
>
> *Erika*: I don't think that's the reason why.

By cutting Brenda off in midsentence, it appeared that Erika had become agitated by Brenda's remarks and therefore chose to dismiss her attempts at further explanation. The perceived attack on her race and gender had increased her emotional stake in the discussion. As a result, she appeared to shut down opinions that did not reinforce her own ideas. Subsequently, others, who appeared much calmer, attempted to provide a satisfactory explanation of why black men date white women. Donna and Paula (another black female participant) provided some sociological and political reasons for the phenomenon:

Paula: I think it's because some think it's like a trophy.

Erika: Exactly. Exactly. It has nothing to do with black women not being intelligent enough.

Donna: It's not a trophy. It's the whole issue of domination and control.

Erika: Exactly.

Paula's remark appeared to demonstrate her awareness of women and "whiteness" in American society as it relates to beauty, achievement, and value. Donna's comment, on the other hand, seemed to suggest her understanding of the distribution of power within interracial, heterosexual relationships, stemming from sociohistorical constructions of black women and white women in American society. In a sense, Donna seemed to be suggesting that black men date white women in an attempt at racial equity. From Erika's comments, it seemed that she was willing to agree with any explanation that supported black women in an attempt to make herself feel better. As the conversation continued, it revolved around Brenda's attempt to clarify her position to the group because she felt that she was being misunderstood. Mark, in exasperation, attempted to give closure to the topic by bringing the conversation back to a discussion of the film:

There's no black women in Kansas. That's all she said.

In effect, it appeared that Mark interpreted Brenda's initial remarks to mean that in certain parts of the country (where Sharif and Stacy plan to move), there were more educated black men than there were black women. Brenda, however, did not acknowledge Mark's support. Therefore, it appeared that she herself did not fully agree with his statement. It seemed as though Brenda had been unwittingly drawn into the debate on interracial dating in the society at large, which consequently forced her to defend herself. Mark's subsequent attempt at closure was ineffective because the conversation continued and his statement was not acknowledged by any other member of the group. Since the topic under discussion involved race and gender issues, it appeared that Mark's comment was not deemed valid because he had no personal stake in the discussion. As a man of mixed racial heritage, Mark was presumably perceived as a nonexpert in that area. Finally, Brenda gave up after several more attempts at explaining her position, although no real common ground was found. It appeared that the topic became so "hot" that it could not be resolved because emotions were too high.

In examining the conversations about the representation of "others," it became apparent that issues pertaining to race and gender were introduced by a person who identified him- or herself as a member of the same ethnic group (and sometimes gender) as the character(s) discussed in the film. Moreover, it appeared that as the discussion about a controversial issue concerning a particular ethnic and/or gender group "heated up," a person from a different ethnic and/or gender group who was in the minority withdrew from the conversation in an attempt to avoid confrontation. Further, none of the participants taking part in the conversation demonstrated a shift in opinion. In fact, as the conversation developed, they became even more entrenched in their views. This seemed to indicate that the controversial topic was extremely "hot" in that the debate was personalized and therefore elicited extreme emotional responses. The discussion of race in a multicultural setting led participants to assert themselves in relation to the social space that they occupy within the larger society, thus illuminating racial tensions between blacks and whites in American society. Donna, in particular, saw herself as both a defender and a teacher of those who did not share her cultural view and subsequently her knowledge about matters concerning the black community. As a result, the opinions of others who were not in agreement with a participant's particular views were dismissed or not heard at all.

Themes

Five overriding themes, derived from the content of the topics mentioned earlier, emerged from the group: meaning making as acquired knowledge, interpretation as inference, interpretation as the responsibility of the viewer, realism as a reflection of life experience and belief, and vested interest in response.

Meaning Making as Acquired Knowledge

Throughout the discussion, participants seemed particularly interested in the film's message as it related to the audience's interpretation of the film. Although most thought that the message was clear—everything you do comes back to you in the end—they were concerned that black teenagers and white audiences would not see the film the way that they did. For instance, Brenda agreed with Donna about the reaction of some black viewers. She added that the film might present a glorified image to the "uneducated viewer." Essentially, they were preoccupied with discussing how others see the film rather than their own feelings about the text. This technique seemed to allow participants to treat the film abstractly since they were unfamiliar with one another and maybe unwilling to expose a part of themselves that might reveal their own insecurities and prejudices. A couple of participants mentioned that they were "different," so they would not see the films the same way that others do. Others distanced themselves from their comments by prefacing their statements with "I'm not saying what I think . . ." and "Other people might think . . ." Both instances suggested that participants were reluctant to directly express their point of view in front of their classmates. In purporting to know the mind-set of other viewers and setting themselves apart from the general audience for the film, participants seemed to reveal their own stereotypes about a particular group. Further, their responses suggested a level of superiority that gave them knowledge about a particular subject unknown to others—how to interpret film. This distancing behavior occurred in comments made by both men and women of various ethnic groups.

Interpretation as Inference

Most of the students seemed to be particularly interested in O-Dog's character. They discussed how he symbolized hope and hopelessness in the community, a theme that surfaced several times during the conversation. Generally, they thought that O-Dog was a product of his environment because he didn't have a family. Several students discussed whether he was capable of changing his behavior. Far less time was devoted to a discussion of Caine's character, which was significant since the story was told from his point of view.

It appeared that Caine's life is presented so completely or straightforwardly that participants understood him to the point that he became the background for other activity (i.e., the actions of O-Dog); that is, Caine's character left less room for interpretation. In the film, Caine's life is traced from beginning to end. Generally, participants seemed to understand why he made the decisions that he made. Through voice-overs, they could hear in Caine's own words the impact that each individual had on his life. In contrast, they were intrigued by O-Dog because of what they did not see or hear about his life. There is less information available about O-Dog than about Caine, which appeared to have left more room for interpretation. Viewers are never allowed to visit O-Dog's family or the place where he lives. The only reference made to his family is in the opening scene, in which the shopkeeper told O-Dog, "I feel sorry for your mother." And O-Dog replied, "What did you say about my mother?"—a comment that prompts him to shoot the shopkeeper to death and rob the convenience store. Further, participants were probably interested in O-Dog because he is the most destructive character in the film. He is the character who perpetrated the most heinous crimes, with seemingly no remorse. Participants discussed why he behaves in such a manner—subsequently attributing it to environmental factors, such as the influx of drugs into the community by those outside the community and more narrowly to a lack of family support created by those conditions. On the surface, O-Dog appears less than "human" in the film because he seems to be one-dimensional and disconnected from mainstream values. In narration, Caine describes O-Dog as "America's nightmare: young, black and didn't give a fuck." However, participants saw him as a tragic character who has little choice in the way that he lives. Brenda articulated it best when she said that she believed "there were times when O-Dog crashed and actually thought about what was going on." It appeared that Brenda could forgive O-Dog for his crimes because he had revealed to her that he is not totally detached from his humanity and is therefore a multidimensional character. Although he never shows remorse for his crimes, Brenda was able to infer from his emotional display after the death of his friends that he could possibly have other feelings as well. As a result, she believed that he had the ability to change. In general, O-Dog's actions were interpreted as less psychotic than they appeared on the surface because participants were able to attribute his behavior to a larger social ill—a racist society. In doing so, they implicitly accepted the directors' sociological view of the problems that contributed to the conditions in that community.

Interpretation as the Responsibility of the Viewer

Although camera technique, quality of acting, and so on were briefly mentioned in the discussion, they were clearly not the main focus of the conversation. It seemed that participants had been drawn into the narrative because they were able to accept the aesthetic construction of the film. However, there was a very brief discussion on the responsibility of directors to make realistic films. Essentially, Donna argued that directors who produce films with minority themes should do so as accurately or as "realistically" as possible:

> Whenever they [the directors] showed where Caine lived with his grandparents . . . I mean, every fifty feet you saw somebody standing out there drinking, standing around smoking pot. You know for people here who have never been . . . and everyone's watching the realism . . . to me that wasn't very realistic.

She went on to say that black filmmakers had a responsibility to the community to be realistic because there were so many negative images about minorities in the media, which had a negative impact on how minorities were perceived in American society. Her comment seemed to suggest that minority filmmakers be held to a higher standard than their mainstream counterparts in order to counteract the negative images in the news media. Donna appeared to be concerned with the way in which negative stereotypes affect social position. Her responses, in general, were far more overtly political than other members of the group. The majority of participants believed that the director had the right to express him- or herself artistically. In support of that argument, Tracie cited films in other genres that did not accurately represent the environment they depicted, such as *Malcolm X* and *Immortal Beloved*.

This discussion reinforced the group's position on the importance of the audience's interpretive knowledge. In effect, participants placed responsibility for interpretation on the viewer rather than the director in the filmmaker/viewer relationship. Group members suggested that it was the audience's responsibility to know what was going on in the film and to draw the "correct" conclusions themselves.

Ironically, however, participants did not always reach the "correct" conclusions. While discussing the impact of the "message" on the audience for the film, Erika, Donna, and Mary seemed to think that O-Dog is the only character to survive the drive-by shooting and thus the hood. In fact, Stacy also survives. Although he is not outside during the incident, he saves Ronnie as gunfire is sprayed throughout the house. As stated earlier, survival and escaping one's environment are common themes in hood films. Stacy is the only one in the group who is not dead or in jail. Further, no one in the group corrected their statements. This misperception seemed to indicate that incorrect information could go unchallenged in a group setting—even among those who believe themselves to be more knowledgeable about the film and the genre's conventions than the general audience.

Realism as a Reflection of Life Experience and Belief

Only a few participants made direct reference to the film's realism. With the exception of Donna, those participants thought that *Menace II Society* was very realistic. The majority of participants who articulated their views based their assessment on their personal experiences. For example, Erika and Donna assessed the film's realistic qualities by comparing it to their personal contact with the kind of environment represented in the film:

Erika: It was very realistic to me. . . . I know people who live in it.

Donna: I've been in projects from California to the East Coast and I have yet to see. . . . Whenever they [the directors] showed where Caine lived with his grandparents . . . I mean, every fifty feet you saw somebody standing out there drinking, standing around smoking pot. You know for people here who have never been . . . and everyone's watching the realism . . . to me that wasn't very realistic.

In response, Tracie seemed to have felt the need to qualify or defend her knowledge about the environment represented in the film because she was speaking to participants with firsthand knowledge of those situations:

> I don't think it's so much a glorified message. It's just the reality. I think you have to do what you have to do to survive. . . . As a white person, I might not live in it, but I am aware.

While she did not have any personal contact with the environment, it seemed that she had knowledge of it through secondhand information, most likely through the media or friends—which suggested a high degree of trust in "authority" and those with whom she shared something in common.

In this case, race was a factor in the manner in which filmic realism was assessed. While the two African American female participants expressed knowledge as cultural insiders, the Caucasian/Jewish female expressed "outsider" knowledge. But, although Donna and Erika used their personal contact with the environment represented in the film as support for their respective arguments, they did not agree on a "reality"—thus suggesting that reality was subjective even among people who share similar experiences. The viewers' judgment of the realism of the film seemed to be based on many complex factors, such as culture, socioeconomic class, gender, and the time and nature of personal contact with the environment depicted.

Vested Interest in Response

During the course of the discussion, several students raised issues related to their gender and/or racial background. Samantha talked about the representation of Latinos in the film. However, her response was not commented on by the other members of the group. Immediately thereafter, Tracie spoke about the representation of white women in the film, which sparked a heated debate. It was more than a little surprising that no one in the group commented on the film's horrific opening sequence in which O-Dog shoots and kills the Korean storekeepers except to state that the shopkeeper's reference to his mother is the only instance in the film where familial connections are made. Nor did the black women in the class comment on the representation of black women in the film.

Based on their responses to various aspects of the film and the lack of responses concerning the opening scene, it can be surmised that while participants in the class spoke freely about some controversial issues, generally they did not feel comfortable enough to introduce into the discussion talk about an ethnic group other than their own. Since the opening sequence is the only scene in the film that depicts violence by a black person against a nonblack person, it might be concluded that interracial violence created more tension in a multicultural setting than the other scenes with black-on-black crime. In a sense, it was a topic that was "too hot" to touch. Moreover, the desire to raise such a controversial topic may have been diminished because there was no one with a vested interest in the discussion since there were no Korean participants in the group. In fact, it may have been counterproductive for black students in the group to address such an issue because the act may have appeared indefensible and would therefore not serve in the best interest of the black students in the group. This suggested that avoidance of controversial issues was an important response strategy.

Further, the decision of participants in the group not to discuss the role of black women in the film seemed to demonstrate the impact of a multicultural group on responses. If we consider that the majority of participants in the group were women and that the group (as a whole) relied heavily on their experiential connection to the film, it would seem that the representation of black women in the film would have merited some discussion. However, it appeared that the women in the group were concerned more with issues relating to race than with those relating to gender in the context of the culturally diverse classroom.

Summary of Response

This section summarizes the group's focus of attention, their critical orientation, their aesthetic distance, and their conflict management and resolution strategies in the discussion of *Menace II Society*.

Focus of Attention
Participants' talk focused largely on the audience for the film. Their generalizations about other viewers of the film appeared to be the

most important topic because it was introduced and reintroduced into the discussion on nine occasions—more than any other topic. Generally, participants were concerned with the impact of the film on uneducated and nonblack viewers. They seemed to agree that different audiences interpret film in diverse ways. Participants' comments seemed to suggest the power that they attributed to the film by highlighting its effect on viewers unlike themselves. Moreover, interpretation was a learned response because group members distinguished between the uneducated and the educated and between blacks (who occupied the primary space in the film) and nonblacks. Their position seemed to suggest their belief in a "correct interpretation" of the text. As suggested earlier, their focus of attention was outside the world of the film.

Critical Orientation
Based on the content of the discussion, it appeared that, generally, members of the group examined the film from a sociological perspective. Participants seemed concerned with society's impact on the characters as well as the audience's response to the film. Their concerns were very much in line with those of the cultural critics who examined the films and their relationship to society at the time of their theatrical release.

Aesthetic Distance
Generally, participants' responses to the film were "warm" in that they seemed to have felt the need to incorporate their life experiences into their responses. The conversation, however, appeared to heat up during the debate on interracial dating, which seemed to touch some of the participants on a personal level—causing them to express what appeared to be intense anger, hurt, and so on.

Conflict Management and Resolution Strategies
During the discussion on interracial dating, participants generally intensified their talk—until Brenda ended the conversation by stating that she would no longer participate because she was having difficulty articulating what she actually meant.

Notes

1. Mary Ann French, "The Brothers Grimm: Menace's Masterminds—Their 'Specialty' Is Violence," *Washington Post*, June 27, 1993, sec. G, p. 4.

2. His comment refers to The Nation of Islam, whose members are known as Black Muslims.

CHAPTER THREE

~

"Money, Power, Respect": Reading *Juice*

I wanted to deal with peer pressure; I think a lot of times this is a force that causes kids to make the choices that they do in their lives—regardless of their economic background, or even racial background. Peer pressure is a real moving force in kids' lives.

—Ernest Dickerson[1]

The second film participants viewed in the hood genre was *Juice* (1992), directed by Ernest Dickerson, who also wrote the story and developed the screenplay with Gerard Brown. *Juice* tells the story of four friends— Q (Omar Epps), Raheem (Khalil Kain), Steele (Jermaine Hopkins), and Bishop (Tupac Shakur)—living in New York City. The film offers an important contribution to the hood genre in that it, along with a few other films, shifts the geographic locale for the representation of urban youth from the West Coast to the East Coast of the United States. And unlike films such as *Straight Out of Brooklyn*, *Just Another Girl on the I.R.T.*, and *Clockers* that focus on Brooklyn, *Juice* is set in Harlem.

The Narrative

The film begins with shots of Q in his bedroom as his mother tries to get him up for school. In Steele's apartment, his father yells, trying to

45

wake him up. At Bishop's apartment, he tells his grandmother good morning and then watches his father stare blankly at the television. Raheem argues with his sister over the bathroom, then tells his mother good-bye as he leaves his apartment. Later, as Bishop walks down the street, several Puerto Rican teenagers corner him in front of a convenience store, telling him that he is psychotic and that he has no "juice." Shortly thereafter, Raheem and Q arrive. Raheem tries to diffuse the situation, but after a brief scuffle, the store's owner appears waving a gun, threatening to shoot them if they don't leave. Everyone scatters. They then meet up with Steele and go to a pool hall with video games. After narrowly escaping the police who raid the place, looking for truants, they shoplift records from a record store so that Q can enter a deejaying competition. While watching a gangster movie on television at Steele's house, they learn through a news report that Blizzard (Darien Berry), a local hoodlum, has been killed in a shoot-out with police. Bishop tells his friends that he is tired of running from everyone—like Blizzard, he said, you have to earn respect.

The next day, Q is selected for the deejay contest. After the audition, he meets Raheem and the others at the basketball court, where Raheem shows them a gun. They decide to rob the convenience store that they have been chased away from. Q is reluctant—telling them that he has to deejay on Saturday night. They plan the robbery around his performance, hoping to use it as their alibi.

During the robbery, Bishop unexpectedly shoots and kills the store's owner. After fleeing the scene, the teenagers end up in an alley and decide to dispose of the gun. When Bishop refuses to give up the gun, Raheem tries to take it from him. Bishop then kills Raheem and threatens to kill anyone who does not follow the plan. They return to the competition in time for Q to perform. During the performance, the police arrive and take Bishop, Steele, and Q in for questioning regarding the death of the convenience store owner. After they are released for insufficient evidence, they attend Raheem's funeral. Q then tries to avoid Bishop, who eventually corners him at school. Bishop threatens to kill Q if he tells anyone what happened.

Later, as Q is having dinner with his girlfriend, Yolanda (Cindy Herron), he gets a call from Steele, who tells him that he is at the pool hall with Bishop and is scared. Before Q arrives, Bishop shoots Steele in an alley. Back at the pool hall, Bishop tells Trip (Samuel L. Jackson), a local hustler, that Q has killed the convenience store owner. Q then tells Trip to tell Bishop that he wants to meet him by the river. When Steele is brought into the hospital, he tells Yolanda (a nurse) that Bishop shot everybody and that he is trying to frame Q. After a fistfight on a rooftop, Bishop accidentally falls over the side of the building. Q catches him but cannot hold on, and Bishop falls to his death. As the crowd looks on, a young man remarks, "You've got the juice now, man," to which Q shakes his head no.

Culturally Diverse Readers

Of the fourteen participants in the study, thirteen were present for the discussion (ten females and three males). Robert was absent, and Carol arrived late. In comparison to the discussion of *Menace II Society*, participation was more evenly distributed—not dominated by a few people. With the exception of Samantha, who did not speak at all, each member of the group made more than one comment on more than one topic. The increased participation by group members (in comparison with the first group discussion) appeared to indicate a higher level of comfort on the part of participants with one another, with the film, and with the topics raised.

The Discussion

I began the discussion by asking participants to tell me what the film was about. Mark, who identified himself as white, black, and Native American, was the first to respond. "It had something to do with peer pressure. Sort of gettin' into the lifestyle of what it takes to have the 'juice.'" After Mark addressed the question, Erika, who categorized herself as black and Filipino, quickly shifted the focus to the development of the characters and the plausibility of the story line (the aesthetic construction of the film), based on Mark's analysis of the film. "I don't know about anybody else, but I felt that the characters and their relationships weren't well developed."

In response to the discussion on the structural deficiencies in the film, in which participants analyzed characters and dialogue, David, a

European American male, introduced the topic of "realism" to the group by comparing his life experiences to the relationships represented in the film. "I grew up in New York City so. . . . What they did. . . . Those kinds of relationships . . . cuttin' school. I understand those relationships where you bag on each other all day long." His entry into the discussion with this comment seemed intended to lend credibility to his interpretation as a nonblack person. After several comments concerning the reality of the characters and the situations that they found themselves in, Mary, an Asian American female, brought the discussion directly back to the specifics of the film in terms of the writing and directing. "I thought that it [Juice] too closely followed a formula."

The comments made on this topic, which centered on Hollywood's penchant for producing predictable films with stock characters, seemed to prompt Mark to introduce into the conversation his experience of seeing the film for the first time in a theater with other audience members and how his concern with what other people thought had changed. After David remarked about the first time he had seen the film in theaters, I asked the rest of the participants if their response had changed from the first time they saw the film. Mark was the only student who stated that his perception of the film had changed. He commented that he was a "bit more relaxed" about seeing Juice in class because the first time he saw the film it was during the time when other "hood" films had been or were being released in the theaters, so he longed for other images. Then, because I hadn't heard yet from Donna, an African American female student, I asked her to tell me what she thought about the film. She returned the conversation to the structure of the film by discussing the underdeveloped characters. "To me it was very cardboardish. . . . Like I said, it followed a formula—the good guy, the bad guy, the guy in the middle who's trying to hold everybody together. And of course you've got the little chubby kid on the side." The conversation continued as Greg, a European American male student, told a personal story that questioned the plausibility of the characters' responses to various situations. After several comments, Brenda, an African American female participant, mentioned how the behavior of the characters was "too premeditated" to be believable or "realistic." More significant, however, she commented that the film could have been more interesting if they had shown more of Bishop's character.

Several members in the group then attempted to talk about other films that may have been closer to what they wanted to see in the theater. Paula (an African American student) brought the conversation back to an analysis of Bishop's life, and this flowed into an examination of the other characters in the film. "What about the point of the father? Showing Bishop's father? He just walked in there and sort of touched him on his shoulder. I didn't get that." Participants then attempted to analyze Bishop on the basis of his family background, and this flowed into an analysis of his friends and their relationship to several other characters in the film in terms of the directing and the script.

Five minutes before the discussion was scheduled to end, I summarized what I thought were some of the major points made by group members—underdeveloped characters, creating an inability to care about their lives, and a story line that lost focus halfway through the film. That statement appeared to prompt Erika to reiterate her displeasure with the progression of the story line and the directing. "It [*Juice*] just sort of shifted focus because he [Bishop] wasn't like the main focus in the beginning." The conversation ended with Mary making a joke about the inappropriateness of the directing and sound track for the scene in which Bishop confronted Q at his locker in school.

Establishing and Changing Topics

Overall, there were nine major shifts in the focus of the conversation on *Juice* and six major topics addressed during that discussion: the film's theme, the aesthetic construction of the film as it related to specific characters and scenes, its "realism," the participant's experiential connection to the subject matter, the reaction of the perceived audience for the film, and the modification of the script to better fulfill the needs of group members. When a topic was categorized as a "theme," it was in reference to discussions focusing on what the film was about. The "aesthetic construction" refers to the general responses concerning the lighting, directing, acting, and so on that were unrelated, specifically to the director. The topics that were categorized as "experiential connections" directly or indirectly placed value on the film on the basis of a participant's own life experience or beliefs. When participants discussed generalizations about the response of other viewers, it was categorized under the heading of "audience." Finally, "altering the script" refers to participants' discussion of alternative story lines as a means to satisfy their "needs" that were not being met by current Hollywood productions.

Both the number of topics and the number of topic changes were significantly lower than the responses for *Menace II Society*. The decrease in the number of topics and topic changes, as compared to the discussion on *Menace II Society*, signified the importance of a particular topic within this discussion—aesthetic construction—to the group as a whole. The number of instances in which participants incorporated one or more of the previous topics raised immediately prior to their response was three out of eight times, which seemed to indicate that a little less than 40 percent of the time, participants maintained at least one of the topics discussed while introducing or reintroducing their own topic(s). Of the nine shifts in topic, Mark was the only participant to change topics more than once. This seemed to suggest that no one person shaped the conversation. Three of the six topics raised (realism, experiential connection, and audience) included talk on issues that were outside the world of the film in that they were only indirectly related to the specifics of the film. This seemed to suggest that participants were equally concerned with the film and its impact on the society at large.

Since I sometimes questioned students during the discussions, occasionally my inquiries resulted in altering the focus of the conversation. One change occurred when I asked if the response of group members to *Juice* had changed since the first time they saw it (after Mary commented on the aesthetic construction of the film). Mark responded to the question first. My question, however, only temporarily altered the discussion, as Donna refocused the conversation on the aesthetic construction of the film. Her response to my attempt to change the course of the discussion seems to further indicate the importance of the topic in the minds of the participants, as the topic was picked up in each subsequent shift for the remainder of the discussion. The overall preoccupation with film technique in the discussion was significant in that it appeared to prohibit most of the participants from connecting to the film in an emotional or experiential way. They were not as concerned with the "message" of the film or the effect of the film on others as in the previous discussion of *Menace II Society*. As a result, the film turned out to be a failure because it did not meet the expectations of its audience.

Point of Conflict: The Effect
of Cinematic Technique on Realism

Throughout the discussion, only one major conflict was expressed by members of the group. Although most of the participants stated that they did not like the film because the characters were not well developed and the plot was not logical, Tracie (a European American female participant), Greg, and David indicated that they liked the film because of its "realism." In other words, things like that happen in real life.

Greg was the only person who explicitly verbalized a shift in position during the course of the conversation. In the earlier stages of the discussion, he commented that the film seemed disjointed. To him, it appeared that *Juice* was in fact two separate films—breaking at the point when Bishop went crazy. His initial analysis was based on the aesthetic construction of the film. Greg stated that after listening to the group discussion, he changed his mind. He argued that the film was plausible and the activities that took place could happen. In that revealing statement, Greg used an analogy from his life experience to justify the actions of the characters in the film. It appeared that during the process of deliberation, in which he was not an active participant, Greg had an opportunity to hear and evaluate both sides of the argument. Subsequently, he appeared to be able to reevaluate his position and then draw a conclusion based on the basis of his new knowledge about the subject matter.

The only other participant who articulated any signs of movement during the discussion was Erika. Initially, she argued that the story wasn't logical. Her shift in opinion was first noticed in her response to Carol, an African American female participant, who stated that the film's use of real rap stars contributed to the implausibility of the story line. Instead of agreeing with the statement because it supported her argument, Erika countered that the film's use of real rap stars was plausible because "you see them all the time in New York." It appeared that Carol's statement caused Erika to draw on her knowledge of living in New York and what she knew to be "real" and then apply that "reality" to her assessment of the film. This suggested the importance of connecting the film to reality for participants because Carol's statement seemed to force Erika to reconsider her position. By the end of the conversation, she conceded that the story line was plausible, although she still had some difficulty with the way the film had been directed.

The main difference between Erika and Greg, other than their gender and ethnicity, was that Erika was an active participant in the conversation and seemed more agitated by the shortcomings of the film than Greg. As an insider who had personal knowledge of rap culture and the environment represented in the film, as explicitly expressed in her comments, Erika appeared to have had more of a vested interest in the characters and situations than Greg. Overall, these shifts in opinion seemed to indicate that the ability to relate the film to some kind of life experience, either directly or indirectly, may have had an impact on the manner in which the film was discussed and the likelihood of whether it was accepted by its audience.

Participants who thought that *Juice* was realistic were in the minority. As a result, the conversation revolved around the aesthetic construction of the film. The participants who thought that the film was realistic spoke only in response to issues raised and on a limited basis. Their defense consisted of a recounting of direct or indirect life experiences (analogies). However, those voices were essentially silent. Generally, there was very little conflict among group members. Although it appeared that each side felt strongly about its position, the discussion was dominated by majority concerns. Overall, participants' responses during this interaction were "lukewarm" in that while they were interested in the issues discussed, they essentially dismissed the film and did not take it seriously.

Themes

Three overriding themes derived from the content of the topics discussed earlier emerged from the group: interpretation as comparison, film as need fulfillment, and realism as a reflection of life experience and value.

Interpretation as Comparison
Participants spent the vast majority of their time trying to make sense of the characters and the scenes. Several of them commented that the

film just didn't make sense, something they attributed largely to its aesthetic construction. In commenting on the scene in which the four friends robbed the convenience store, Brenda said,

> It was all so premeditated. . . . I mean, in everyday life, or people that do these things, they don't sit down and plan to rob a store. . . . I don't know too many people that are thugs who say that "we're gonna go and beat this guy up on such and such a day," unless something has already been done to provoke it.

By comparing a scene in the film to her real life "insider" experience, Brenda appeared to have been able to dismiss the film entirely.

Several other participants commented that they either did not feel connected to the characters or did not believe their relationships. Erika, the most vocal member throughout the discussion, seemed the most annoyed with the film as she compared it to other films in the genre:

> I don't know about anybody else, but I felt that the characters and their relationships weren't well developed. I mean like in *Boyz n the Hood* and *Menace*, I felt like I had a general understanding of the characters and maybe cared about them in a certain way.

By comparing *Juice* to other films in the genre, Erika seemed to suggest that there was a standard that films should adhere to, based on her knowledge of "hood" films and filmmaking in general. She appeared to have a definite idea of what was acceptable when representing certain issues and film genres. Donna, who admitted to seeing the film at least three or four times because someone else wanted to watch it, said that she didn't like the movie at all because it was not well developed. Further, for her, the film seemed to offer only stock characters found in most Hollywood films.

Overall, her comments seemed to suggest that a negative perception of a film does not preclude one from watching it more than once. There were, apparently, mitigating factors, such as one's relationship with others, that determined the viewing experience. Moreover, Donna expected the film to differentiate itself from the standard fare she had seen in theaters. Like Erika, her response seemed to have been based on her understanding of films and filmmaking. Similarly, Mark commented that the characters were not "human," or multidimensional.

Finally, participants who articulated their views were in general agreement about the representation of women in the film. Several questioned the logic and plausibility of Q's girlfriend. While they agreed that her role in the story was superfluous, there was disagreement over the plausibility of Q's dating an older, professional woman. In defense of that relationship, Donna stated that she could relate to that experience because she was an older woman, although overall she did not think that the film was believable. Donna's life experience seemed to determine her acceptance of that particular scene. Her response was similar to Erika's, who also appeared to dismiss the film in its entirety, although she was able to relate to a particular scene. Therefore, it appeared that the life experiences of the viewer, in relation to the events and characters depicted in the film, played a major role in how a participant interpreted the film.

Black American pariticipants consistently discussed the film in terms of its aesthetic construction. They considered the script, the acting, and the directing. As a group, they did not appear to be concerned with what "others" thought because they felt that *Juice* was severely flawed and was therefore not an effective film. Similarly, they did not articulate an interest in issues concerning the film's message. Notably, their views were in congruence with those held by many critics in the popular press.

Film as Need Fulfillment
A few participants who voiced their dissatisfaction with the film made suggestions on how to make it work. As stated earlier, some of them advised making the characters more "human." Specifically, Donna suggested showing Bishop's inner turmoil. In a conversation that included Mark, Erika, and Donna, an alternative story line was proposed:

> *Mark*: I was thinking about something that might be a little bit more interesting that I haven't seen quite as much. . . . Just like a story about the friends . . . the four friends and their friendship. . . . Just to examine. I mean, they could all be doin' something, whatever, deejaying, or whatever. I don't know. . . . I've never seen a story about . . .
>
> *Erika*: Relationships.

Mark: Yeah. African American.

Donna: A male African American.

In rewriting the premise of the film, participants seemed to have been indicting mainstream cinema as well as the filmmaker under discussion. They were reiterating their desire to see more "human" or multidimensional characters. This seemed to suggest that their interpretation was related to their experience with the representation of African Americans in mainstream media, which they found stereotypical. Therefore, they reworked the narrative to fulfill their own needs as a cultural group since the participants engaged in that discussion identified themselves as at least in part black.

Realism as a Reflection of Life Experience and Value
Of the participants who believed that the film was realistic, the Caucasian students appeared to be the most vocal. Tracie commented that she liked the film the first time, but she was more disturbed by it this time because now she saw the "hopelessness in the characters." Moreover, she stated that she knew people who could be in that situation. For her, the film was very realistic because now she had had personal contact with the kinds of people depicted—although she did not really know anyone who had been involved in such activity:

> I've seen it before, and I felt very differently about it this time. . . . I really liked it the first time I saw it, and I understood it and everything. This time, I don't think I liked it as much, 'cause I think it scared me a little more. I think it was a bit too close. . . . I've never been in that situation, as far as the story line, but I do know a couple people that that could be.

As an "outsider," Tracie's perspective had shifted within that boundary because she had met people unlike herself and made assumptions about their similarities to the characters in the film. So, although she was an outsider, she seemed to believe that she had intimate knowledge of the kinds of people represented in the film. Further, her response suggested that attitudes can shift over time with the introduction of an experience or a person "close to home."

David stated that he liked *Juice* better than *Boyz n the Hood*. He argued that the film was realistic because he had had direct contact with the kinds of people and situations represented in the film—suggesting the universality of the narrative.

> I grew up in New York City. . . . I understand the whole scam they're trying to run. I like that aspect of it. . . . It represents a situation that I have been in or close to several times.

On several occasions, he defended the film and the characters to his classmates on the basis of his direct personal experiences. Unlike the other participants, he was clearly an insider who seemed to be able to appreciate the criminal activity in the film.

Greg, who early on stated that the second half of *Juice* seemed unrealistic, rethought his position:

> I was sitting here thinking to myself. . . . I mean, I didn't see any of my friends do anything like that, but I can recall a lot of times when, on another level, like guys would jump, beat someone up, or whatever, for no other reason than to just do it. And I always sit there thinking, "What are these people thinking?"

Greg went on to tell the story of two affluent men fighting over a parking space in the Hamptons,[2] asserting his position as an extreme outsider in order to let the group know that he could only indirectly relate to the situations under discussion. Apparently, the film was realistic for participants who classified themselves as Caucasian, who used their direct or indirect life experiences to argue that the film was realistic. Subsequently, they spent most of their time defending the film to the rest of the group. All the participants, however, seemed to believe that realism was an important criterion for judging the merit of the film.

Summary of Response

This section summarizes the focus of attention of the group, their critical orientation, their aesthetic distance, and their conflict management and resolution strategies for the discussion on *Juice*.

Focus of Attention

Participants clearly spent the majority of their time discussing the aesthetic construction of the film. Generally, they thought that the characters and their situations were not well developed. As a result, they did not think that the film was very realistic. Their central question appeared to be why *Juice* did not work as a film. In general, the themes addressed—interpretation as comparison, film as need fulfillment, and realism as a reflection of life experience and value—were directly related to the film itself.

Critical Orientation

Participants were most interested in the technical qualities of the film, such as the acting, directing, and the manner in which the narrative unfolded. As a result, they brought a knowledge of aesthetic criticism to their interpretation of the text.

Aesthetic Distance

With few exceptions, the participants' emotional tone seemed rather "warm" during the discussion of *Juice*. Generally, group members felt that *Juice* failed as a film. They seemed annoyed that the story of the young men was not effectively told.

Conflict Management and Resolution Strategies

The general strategy for dealing with conflicts within the group appeared to be the intensification of statements in the face of actual and unanticipated rebuttal. At points of conflict throughout the discussion, participants routinely provided additional information about the topic under discussion in an attempt to support their points.

Notes

1. Jacquie Jones, "Peer Pressure," *Black Film Review* 7, no. 2 (1993): 24.
2. The Hamptons is a very affluent part of Long Island, New York.

~

CHAPTER FOUR

"Increase the Peace":
Reading *Boyz n the Hood*

They [the media] don't want to deal with the fact that the high
crime and murder rates are directly related to the illiteracy problem, the homeless problem, problems in the American educational system. . . . Everybody else copies young black men. If I
reach them, everything else will fall into place.[1]

—John Singleton

The third and final film participants screened from the hood genre was
Boyz n the Hood (1991), written and directed by John Singleton. The
film traces the lives of three black males—Tre (Cuba Gooding Jr.),
Ricky (Morris Chestnut), and Doughboy (Ice Cube)—in South-Central
Los Angeles from childhood through their teenage years.

The Narrative

The film opens with the following statistic: "One out of every twenty-
one Black American males will be murdered in their lifetime. Most will
die at the hands of another Black male."

The scene then abruptly shifts to show a "Stop" sign. Later, a ten-
year-old Tre (Desis Arne Hines II) gets into a fight with a classmate. As
a result, his mother, Reva (Angela Bassett), has decided to send him to

live with his father, Furious Styles (Laurence Fishburne). Tre's mother tells him that he is going to live with his father because she does not want to see him dead, in jail, or drunk in front of a liquor store. As Reva drops him off, she promises to come back for him after she gets a better job and a better place to stay.

The first night, Furious explains the rules of the house to Tre—which includes all the chores he has to do. After they go to bed, Furious hears someone trying to break into the house. He then fires his gun through the door. Tre and Furious sit and wait for almost an hour for the police to arrive. Furious then describes to the two officers what happened. The black officer tells him that since no one is hurt and nothing is missing, there is no need to file a report. He goes on to tell Furious that it is too bad that he didn't get him because "there would be one less nigger out here in the streets to worry about." After Furious sends Tre into the house, the officer asks Furious if there is something wrong. Furious tells the officer that "there is something, it's just too bad that he doesn't know what it is."

The next day, Tre meets with his friends Ricky (Donovan McCrary) and Doughboy (Baha Jackson), half brothers who are on their way to see another friend, Chris (Kenneth A. Brown). Chris then takes them to see a dead body. As they examine the body, some teenage boys take Ricky's football. When Doughboy tries to get the ball back, he is taunted and kicked in the stomach. Later, one of the teens gives him back the ball. That afternoon, Furious takes Tre fishing. Furious talks to Tre about the importance of being a leader instead of a follower. Then they discuss the responsibility that goes along with having sex. On the way home, they see Doughboy and Chris being taken away in a police car for stealing.

Seven years later, at a barbecue for Doughboy, who has just gotten out of jail, Chris (Redge Green) is in a wheelchair—the victim of a shooting. Ricky is a teenage father. When Tre arrives, Ricky and Doughboy's mother, Mrs. Baker (Tyra Ferrell), asks him to talk to Doughboy about staying out of trouble. While playing cards, someone asks Doughboy what he did in jail. Doughboy replies that he worked out and read. His friends laugh.

Tre, who has been avoiding his girlfriend Brandi (Nia Long) for five days, goes over to her house to try and convince her that they should have sex. She tells him that she wants to wait until she is married because she is Catholic. Later that night, while Tre is on the phone with Brandi, Tre's mother calls from an upscale apartment. After speaking to Tre, she tells Furious that she wants Tre to come and live with her. Furious tells her that it is Tre's decision now because he is a grown man. Meanwhile, a college recruiter from the University of Southern California (Hudhail Al-Amir) visits Ricky to talk about a football scholarship. He tells Ricky that all he has to do is score 700 on the SATs to get into college. On the front porch, Doughboy and his boys are also talking about what it would be like to go to college. On Saturday, Tre, Brandi, and Ricky take the test. When it is over, Ricky and Tre visit Furious at his financial loan business. He takes them to Compton— a neighborhood undergoing gentrification, as evidenced by a large sign indicating new construction. As a crowd gathered, he explains that drugs, guns, and liquor stores are in the community and bringing property values down because "they" want "us" to kill ourselves.

Later that evening, Tre and Ricky drive to Chrenshaw Boulevard— where groups of teenagers are hanging out. Doughboy, Chris, and two other friends are already there, discussing the existence of God. Then Ferris (Raymond D. Turner), a local gang leader, bumps into Ricky. When Ricky stands up to him, Doughboy shows his gun, and Ferris's gang backs down. Shortly thereafter, Ferris pulls out a machine gun and fires it into the air. The crowd scatters. On the way home, Tre and Ricky are stopped by Officer Coffey (Jesse Ferguson), the same cop who responded to the break-in at their house several years earlier. As Officer Coffey holds a gun to Tre's head, tears stream down his face. When Tre arrives at Brandi's house, he breaks down and cries. Brandi has been doing her homework to the sound of gunfire and the glare of helicopter surveillance lights. Subsequently, the two end up sleeping together. The next day, in Mrs. Baker's front yard, Ricky and Doughboy get into a fight after Doughboy states that Ricky always receives preferential treatment since they have different fathers. Tre and Ricky then leave for the store as the mailman delivers their SAT scores. On the way home, they spot Ferris and his gang, so they run. Against Tre's better judgment, they decide to split up. Meanwhile, Doughboy, sensing that something is wrong, goes looking for Ricky, who has slowed down in the alley to look at his lottery ticket. By the time Doughboy and his gang get there, Ricky is already dead. Tre and Doughboy then take Ricky's bloodied body home. Through a stream of tears, Doughboy's mother continuously hits him, yelling that he caused it to happen.

As Tre and Doughboy drive around looking for the guys who killed Ricky, Tre suddenly asks Doughboy to let him out of the car. Meanwhile, when Mrs. Baker opens Ricky's SAT scores, she realizes that he had made the 700 points needed to get into college. Later, Doughboy shoots and kills Ferris and his gang.

The next morning, Doughboy visits Tre on his front porch. He tells him that he understands why he got out of the car because he should not have been there in the first place. He tells Tre that the news shows all the violence that happens in foreign countries, but it didn't show anything about his brother. Before Doughboy ritualistically spills out his beer, he says, "Either they don't know, don't show, or don't care about what's going on in the hood." In written narration, the audience learns that Doughboy is murdered two weeks later and that Tre and Brandi are attending Morehouse and Spelman colleges, respectively. Simultaneously, the audience is visually left with the image of Doughboy dissolving into nonexistence as Tre sits on the front porch. *Boyz* ends with the title of the film and the words "Increase the Peace" in white on a black background.

Culturally Diverse Readers

On the day of the discussion, all fourteen participants (ten women and four men) were present. With the exception of Soo, who spoke only at the very end of the conversation when I asked participants to talk about the genre in general, everyone was actively involved in the discussion. No one person dominated the conversation.

The Discussion

I began the conversation about *Boyz n the Hood* by reminding participants of the comments made by several students during the discussion of *Juice*—which compared *Juice* to *Boyz n the Hood*. Some participants mentioned that *Boyz n the Hood* was a better movie, so I asked them to explain why they believed that to be the case. Brenda, an African

American female, was the first to respond to the question. She told the group how moved she was by *Boyz* because the situation depicted in the film existed in society. Brenda commented that she had had the same reaction the first time she saw the film. In the next comment, Erika, who identified herself as Filipino and black, also spoke about her emotions concerning the film—then and now. However, she moved the conversation further by commending the director for doing a good job. "I thought that the way that we got to see them [Tre, Ricky, and Doughboy] grow up . . . from childhood. . . . I just thought that was a really responsible thing to do." After commenting on the film's director and recounting the first time he saw the film, Mark stated that he liked *Menace II Society* more than *Boyz n the Hood* because the characters in *Menace II Society* seemed more "hopeless."

After a brief discussion on the theme of the film, the conversation evolved into a discussion of Doughboy when Brenda stated that his behavior should not be characterized in terms of hope or hopelessness. I then asked participants if they agreed with Brenda's description of Doughboy, and several responded that they did not. The discussion continued as participants discussed Ricky and Doughboy. After analyzing the behavior of various characters in relationship to the two brothers, Mark, who categorized himself as black, white, and Native American, changed the topic when he commented that the director must have drawn on his own personal experience in developing the scene in which Tre attempted to talk Brandi (his girlfriend) into having sex with him because it was so well done. "That was so perfect. I know that John Singleton had that conversation." Then Mark abruptly shifted the conversation back to an analysis of Ricky by posing a question concerning his behavior at the moment he was shot and killed. "But could I step back to Ricky one second? Why didn't he jump? Or why didn't he run?" In analyzing the scene in which Ricky was shot, students compared his reaction to what they or other people in those neighborhoods would do in that situation. After a few exchanges, Erika abruptly shifted the conversation back to a discussion of the film's theme as it related to Doughboy. "And back to Doughboy. I don't think he didn't have hope or desire. I just think he was sort of . . . just so used to being perceived in a certain way, and he tried to fight against it, but he would always end up accepting it." After they seemed to have

exhausted the topic, I asked if any of them had just seen the film for
the first time. No one answered. So I asked again, "Everyone's seen it
before?" Then they laughed. So I asked participants to tell me what
they remembered about the first time they saw the film. Erika said she
cried, which indicated her emotional connection to the film. The
other women in the class answered almost in unison, "Me too." Then
I said, "Okay, the women cried. What did the men do?" David, a white
male student, began to tell me about his experience of seeing the film
in Los Angeles—which focused the conversation on the shootings outside some theaters. After I told the group that the film had been pulled
from several theaters because of violence following its airing, I asked
them why they thought that the shootings occurred. Mary commented
that the trailers advertising the film may have contributed to the violent behavior. Later I asked whether they were aware that in an adver-
tisement for one of the films a gun was airbrushed out in order not to
incite violent behavior.[2] Donna, an African American woman, cited
other films whose advertising displayed guns. She remarked, "That's
strange, because when you see other posters for other action movies
you see the stars portrayed with guns or whatever particular weapon—
like The Terminator." Tracie (a European American female participant)
commented that the distributors were making an assumption about the
audience. "I don't think that you would see thirty-year-old, middle-
class, white people seeing Juice." When I asked her to clarify her statement, she said, "It's different if you see Clint Eastwood with a gun."
The conversation continued as participants discussed the effect of violent images on the target audience for a film. Brenda then slightly
shifted the focus of the conversation by talking about her emotional
connection to other films. "I mean, 'cause I know honestly speaking
. . . I don't mean to offend anybody [but] after I saw Roots, I was rude
to a lot of white people." After Greg, who identified himself as European American, discussed his emotions after viewing films outside the
genre, I asked Samantha, a Hispanic female, to tell me how a "positive
message" might be received by the audience for the film. My question
was raised in response to her previous comment. She replied, "Sometimes messages are lost. Like if a certain scene touches you. . . . Or you
can end up focusing on the faults of the movie, rather than the overall
picture." In addressing the "message" of the film in relation to its audi-

ence, David commented, "We all grabbed a message from it, but to an eighteen-year-old kid who's dropped out of high school and lives that lifestyle, who's in the position of Doughboy, what message is he walking away with?" Then Mark, after explicitly acknowledging the remarks about the message and the audience, slightly shifted the focus of the conversation to his experiential connection to the kinds of people represented in hood films. He argued that people who live like Doughboy, Ricky, and Tre seemed to have received a positive message from films like *Menace II Society*.

In an attempt to give closure to the discussion, I then asked participants to give me their general impressions of the genre. Erika was the first to respond. Generally, participants discussed the message, the director, realism, the audience, the need for images like this, whether they liked the genre, and personal background information.

Establishing and Changing Topics

Overall, there were fourteen major shifts in topic during the course of the discussion. Ten topics were introduced or reintroduced by seven of the fourteen participants present; they were the film's "realistic" qualities based on participants' own life experience or beliefs; the participants' emotional connection or feelings about the film; the aesthetic construction of the film in terms of the acting and the script; the ability of the director to portray the lives of the characters; the film's theme; the narrative content of the film, specifically the behavior of its characters; the audience for the film; the film's "message"; the experience of participants as it related to the kind of people or environment represented in the film; and the controversy surrounding the advertising for the film.

The number of occasions in which participants incorporated one or more of the previous topics raised immediately prior to their response was nine out of thirteen times, which seemed to indicate that nearly 70 percent of the time, participants maintained at least one of the topics discussed while introducing or reintroducing their own topic(s) (a figure that was similar to that found in the discussion on *Menace II Society*). Further, five of the ten topics raised during the discussion referred primarily to the social world outside the world of the film (realism, emotional connection, audience, experiential connection, and advertising) in that they were only indirectly related to the specifics of the film. As in the discussion on *Juice*, this seemed to suggest that participants were equally as concerned with the social issues raised by the film as with the narrative of the film itself. Of the participants who established or changed topics, Brenda, Erika, and Mark seemed to have had the greatest impact on the flow of the conversation. Brenda and Erika raised at least one of the same issues on more than one occasion. Generally, participants seemed most concerned with discussing their emotional connection to the film, the audience for the film and hood films in general, and the film's "message."

While the flow of the conversation was generally determined by participants, I changed the course of the discussion on four occasions by asking probing questions in an attempt to keep the conversation moving. The first shift occurred when I asked participants to tell me about the first time they saw *Boyz n the Hood*—which elicited an emotional response from Erika. The second instance occurred when I asked participants why they thought the shootings occurred outside some theaters. That question elicited a response that focused on the advertising campaigns for the films. The third change occurred when I told participants how the advertisements for *Juice* had been changed. My fourth question was in response to an issue raised earlier in the discussion by Samantha regarding a statement she made about "positive messages." Her response to my question on the "message" of the film introduced a topic that resurfaced two more times before the end of the discussion.

It appears that the conversation was essentially two discussions—changing almost immediately after I asked participants a question. During the first half of the discussion, participants seemed most concerned with their personal relationship to the film (e.g., its "realism" based on their emotional connection to the film and praise for the writer and director in terms of the development of characters). During the second half of the discussion, participants seemed most interested in outside connections to the film (e.g., the message of the film as interpreted by a particular audience). After Brenda's response, my question to Samantha again brought the discussion back to a more global view of hood films—their relationship to society—which was maintained throughout the remainder of the discussion.

Points of Conflict

Generally, throughout the course of the conversation, there were no major conflicts. Participants seemed to work together to analyze the behavior of the characters who exhibited questionable behavior. When a concern was expressed, it was immediately answered by another member of the group. If another person could provide some insight into the discussion, he or she did so. As a result, participants for the most part acknowledged the validity of interpretations made by their fellow group members even if they did not agree with those interpretations. In other words, they appeared to acknowledge the other side of the argument whether they agreed with it or not.

For example, Cathy (a European American female participant) stated that she could not understand why Brandi would sleep with Tre, given her strong religious convictions. Erika and several other women commented that things like that happen, even with people who are very religious, when they are in love. While Cathy admitted that she understood their comment, she stated that she could not accept that a devout Catholic would change her mind so quickly about something so serious. Mark then shifted the discussion to the scene's relationship to the real life of the director.

In Cathy's case, the lack of support from the group and her inability to provide additional information about the point under discussion caused the conversation to quickly die out. However, the lack of intensity with which the point was debated appeared also to be indicative of a lack of interest on the part of the participants. It seemed clear from the discussion that participants were generally in agreement on their response to the film. Generally, the response was "warm" in that it revolved around the articulation of emotional feelings.

The only significant difference in opinion occurred when I asked participants to explain why they thought that violence occurred at some of the theaters exhibiting hood films. Although almost every participant gave a slightly different response, however, they listened to and were respectful of others' ideas. Each participant stated his or her opinion and then listened to the opinion of the others, incorporating what they deemed useful and ignoring what was not. Interestingly, their discussion mirrored arguments expressed in mainstream media at the time of the film's release.

In analyzing the responses of audience members who displayed anti-social behavior at the theaters, participants engaged one another by asking questions that challenged each other's assumptions. Additionally, every participant (with the exception of Soo) had a theory concerning the incidents. Therefore, the debate lasted longer than other points of conflict, which seemed to indicate a higher level of interest in the topic. Further, throughout the discussion there was a constant exchange of ideas that challenged the group. Although participants did not reach a consensus, the conversation shifted focus when Robert added that a positive "message" did not always ensure a positive response. Since no one could really dispute that statement, they began to concentrate on the "message" of *Boyz n the Hood* by analyzing the characters through the eyes of the people who lived the kind of life that was represented on the screen.

Themes

The following section describes the content of the focus group discussion. Three overriding themes, derived from the topics discussed earlier, emerged from the group: interpretation as negative identification, meaning making as the circulation of ideas, and realism as a reflection of emotional attachment.

Interpretation as Negative Identification

In the first half of the discussion, participants were primarily concerned with examining the reactions of two of the main characters—Ricky and Doughboy—to particular situations. Generally, they attempted to understand the behavior of the two characters by putting themselves in their shoes. For example, the group discussed why Ricky did not run when he was being chased by members of a gang. After several minutes, they concluded that Ricky was a dreamer and was therefore not street-smart enough to know the danger he was in. Generally, they attributed Ricky's behavior to his lack of street smarts, while Doughboy was considered a victim of his environment.

From their conversation, it appeared that participants were more concerned with the characters of Ricky and Doughboy than with others because they were the furthest away from themselves in terms of goals;

therefore, there was a need to understand the motivations for their behavior. By the end of the film, Tre and his girlfriend were the only characters to make it out of the ghetto and go to college because of the positive role models in their lives. Both Ricky and Doughboy were killed
because they did not have the same foundation. Although many of the
participants considered themselves insiders, it seemed as though they
were not close enough to fully comprehend what it was like to be faced
with the choices that Ricky and Doughboy saw for themselves. Their
comments seemed to suggest that interpretation in this instance was related to the degree of experiential connectedness to the characters.

Meaning Making as the Circulation of Ideas

In the second half of the discussion, participants were concerned with
how other people viewed the film—particularly, nonblack and uneducated viewers. The group seemed to position itself outside the society
at large. Generally, they did not think that others would see the film
the way they did. As in the discussion on *Menace II Society*, participants
appeared to set themselves apart from the general public.

Participants also addressed the issue of modified advertising campaigns for some of the films after I introduced the topic. Tracie argued
that the advertising attracted a certain kind of audience—those who
were more likely to engage in violent behavior. She attempted to distance herself from her remarks, however, which seemed to indicate
that she believed that her statement might not be accepted by the
group as a whole. In her comment, she intimated that the race of the
audience for the films caused distributors to modify the ad campaigns
for some of the films. She stated that a violent ad aimed at inner-city
youth will not have the same impact as a violent ad aimed at middle-
class white people:

> I don't think that you would see thirty-year-old, middle-class, white peo-
> ple seeing *Juice*. I'm saying that that's probably why they pulled the
> poster. . . . I'm not saying what I think. I'm saying what the media . . .
> why they pulled it.

Drawing on her perspective as a middle-class white person, Tracie
seemed to have been suggesting that she was able to speak for the media

because they represented the mainstream culture of which she is a part. In this instance, apparently, she had positioned herself as an insider, although she understood that in doing so she must distance herself in order to deflect any criticism. On the other hand, Erika argued that the trailers took violent scenes out of context:

> They take certain scenes out of context and it just looks like violent, violence.

In effect, Erika seemed to blame the media or, more broadly, mainstream society for the negative images of African Americans. However, Donna stated that the particular audience the film attracted was prone to violence:

> The movies probably just appealed to that type of people. And when they went there, they're just acting on their natural . . . the way they normally behave. You know what I mean? . . . They didn't just come there to fight. That's just their personality. And when they got there, they just acted accordingly.

In contrast, Brenda and Greg thought that hood films evoked a certain emotional response in audience members in general. Therefore, they did not blame the films for the audience's responses because many films have evoked strong emotional responses. Brenda said,

> I mean, 'cause I know honestly speaking . . . I don't mean to offend anybody [but] after I saw *Roots*, I was rude to a lot of white people. It's just a feeling that you have. . . . Like after I saw *The Color Purple*, the first thing I wanted to do was go and call my sister. . . . It's just that feeling that you walk away with. And you think about it.

Greg stated,

> I think the movie definitely brings out violence in people. You know . . . like when I go see *Rocky*, I come out like I want to box or something. And, like I know a lot of people in my school seem to have a copy of *New Jack City*. Like, when people finish watching they want to go out, like in a few hours, and be like drug dealers or something.

By introducing other films outside of the genre, Greg and Brenda seemed to have been acknowledging that it is the nature of the film to engender strong emotional responses. Generally, their comments seemed to suggest that viewers draw on the totality of their experiences with film to aid in interpretation.

On the other hand, David, who saw the film in Los Angeles, suggested that the audience for the film consisted of rival gang members who grew impatient from waiting in line at the theater:

> You have Doughboys and the flip side, who waited all day to see it [*Boyz n the Hood*]. It was a crazy atmosphere. And you didn't feel any more relaxed when the lights went out. No more relaxed. It was a fairly real representation.

His firsthand experience seems to have aided him in his interpretation of the film and its audience. Mark supported David when he argued that the location of the movie theaters brought existing rivalries together.

> I don't think the movie [*Boyz n the Hood*] had anything to do with it. I'm figuring that people ran into a few people that they might have had problems with. Or they got frustrated 'cause they were in line too long. . . . I think it was probably just rivalries that people didn't know about.

The difference in the two responses was that David appeared to draw on his specific experience at the theatrical showing of the film, while Mark appeared to draw on his understanding of gang life obtained from other sources. Both, however, seemed to place blame on a specific segment of society, not on the audience as a whole. Overall, it appeared that by introducing into the conversation the controversy about the advertising campaigns, I caused some participants to rethink their positions on the audience's responsibility in the interpretive process, as first articulated during the discussion on *Menace II Society*, in which the onus to achieve the "correct" interpretation was on the audience itself.

Realism as a Reflection of Emotional Attachment
In general, participants routinely mentioned how "realistic" they thought the film was as they compared it to how people behave in real

life. However, unlike in the discussions of the other films, they offered almost no personal stories to support their statements. Instead, several students commented on how well developed the characters were and linked this to their feelings about the film's "realism." In response to a comment made by Cathy concerning why Doughboy was treated differently from his half brother Ricky, for example, Erika stated,

> And that goes to show how well the characters were developed. Like Ricky and Doughboy's mother . . . I thought that was an excellent character, 'cause she was a real . . . a real woman and she . . . her emotions were real.

In this comment, Erika seemed to use her knowledge of how a woman would react to the death of her son as a basis for assessing realism in the film.

While it was possible that participants had exhausted accounts of their personal experiences in previous discussions, it is also likely that many of the participants felt a deeper emotional connection to the film than to the other films in the study. Erika seemed to have been drawn into the narrative because she believed that her emotions were similar to those of the characters. Several students commented how moved they were by the film because it was so "realistic." From the dialogue, it appeared that the ability to feel the emotion of the characters was tied to each participant's sense of realism in hood films.

Summary of Response

This section summarizes the group's focus of attention, their critical orientation, their aesthetic distance, and their conflict management and resolution strategies for the discussion on *Boyz n the Hood*. Because of the dramatic impact of my introducing into the discussion the advertising campaigns for the films, only the responses made by participants prior to my changing the topic were used to construct the summaries.

Focus of Attention
Generally, during the first half of the discussion, participants were concerned with discussing topics specifically related to the narrative con-

tent of the film. They were particularly interested in understanding why Doughboy and Ricky made the decisions that they made. This was reflected in the themes that emerged from the discussion: interpretation as negative identification, meaning making as the circulation of ideas, and realism as a reflection of emotional attachment.

Critical Orientation

Based on the content of the discussion, participants seemed to take a psychosocial approach to the film in that they appeared to put themselves in the shoes of the characters and their circumstances in order to understand their behavior.

Aesthetic Distance

When I asked participants to tell me what they thought the first time they saw *Boyz n the Hood*, many of the female students stated that they cried. David appeared to see the question as an invitation to tell the group about his experience of seeing the film in South-Central Los Angeles. Generally, their discussion of the film was "warm" in that participants felt the need to express their emotions about the physical and social space that the characters occupied during the discussion.

Conflict Management and Resolution Strategies

Generally, there were no significant conflicts during the discussion. Participants listened to the comments made by other group members and merely offered their opinions. Their position was one of acceptance in that after expressing their own point of view, they or the group moved on to another topic.

Notes

1. Alan Light, "Not Just One of the Boyz," *Rolling Stone*, September 5, 1991, 73-75.

2. The film for which a gun was airbrushed out was *Juice* (1992). "The film's original poster reportedly showed the villain of the story holding a gun—until the studio decided the gun might seem too provocative and airbrushed it away." David Sterrit, "Streetwise Film *Juice* Stirs Up Bad Publicity," *Christian Science Monitor*, February 11, 1992, 11.

CHAPTER FIVE

~

Negotiated Meanings

Since this was not the first time that I had shown films in the hood genre, the discussions that followed the screenings of the films were not entirely surprising. What was interesting was how ideas were exchanged throughout the discussion, specifically how the films, the immediate social context, and their own personal characteristics allowed participants to speak rather freely for such a lengthy period of time (approximately forty-seven minutes for *Menace II Society*, forty-one for *Juice*, and forty-five for *Boyz n the Hood*) with varying but relatively little interference from me.

In the pages that follow, I synthesize the material presented in the chapters on *Menace II Society*, *Juice*, and *Boyz n the Hood*. The purpose of this is to explore the role of the films, the reader (viewer), and the immediate social context (the composition of the group during the discussion) in shaping the responses of participants. For each section, I looked at where participants focused their attention, what critical orientation (or analytical lens) was used to examine each film, and their aesthetic distance from a particular text.

The Role of the Films in Shaping Response

The dialogue during the group discussions was a clear indication that the films played a significant role in shaping response within the group setting. Generally, participants focused their attention on the social world outside the film during the discussion of *Menace II Society*, concentrating on the audience for the film. During the discussions of *Juice* and *Boyz n the Hood*, however, their responses focused on the world inside the film. For *Juice*, that meant that participants were concerned with the aesthetic construction of the film. Responses made by participants during the discussion for *Boyz n the Hood* were centered on analyzing two of the main characters. The differences in their responses can be partially attributed to the features of the texts, specifically the representation of violence. *Menace II Society* was the most graphic of the three films in terms of language and imagery. The violence in the film was cold and spontaneous in that it occurred at any time to anyone. There were several instances in the film in which violence played a major role in the development of the characters. The most striking example was the opening sequence of the film in which O-Dog shoots and kills the Korean shopkeeper and his wife. In narration, Cain states, "Went into the store just to get a beer. Came out an accessory to murder and armed robbery. It was funny like that in the hood sometimes. You never knew what was going to happen or when." In another instance, Caine witnesses his father nonchalantly shoot a man to death because his friend balked that he owed him money. In yet another incident, O-Dog, at point-blank range, shoots and then kicks a crack addict who offers to perform a sexual act as payment for drugs. Equally shocking is the almost nonreaction of O-Dog's two friends, who don't seem particularly bothered by this act of brutality, illustrating the numbness felt by the characters in the film to spontaneous acts of violence in their community. Consequently, the graphic nature of those scenes may have made it difficult for participants to directly relate to or identify with the characters and their situations. The highly stylized depiction of violence throughout the film (e.g., the use of slow motion when Caine is shot as his life flashes before his eyes—representing not only a wasted life but also a life lived from which one could not escape) intensifies the brutality of the act. In this sense, participants may have been disturbed by the film's graphic depiction of violence, which was read as "realism." Therefore, they discussed *Menace* from a distanced perspective by talking about the response—or the imagined responses—of economically and racially diverse "others." In addition, the violence in *Menace* was cyclical. Caine shows Ronnie's son how to use a gun, just as Pernell showed him. This tradition of passing down to the younger generation most likely caused participants some discomfort because the violence is not restricted to *Menace* itself but continues long after the audience stops watching.

The representation of violence in *Juice* was quite different. First, with regard to the main characters in the film, it was premeditated. Bishop, Steele, Q, and Raheem plan an armed robbery of a convenience store. Bishop deviates from the plan, to the surprise of the others, when he kills the shopkeeper. More important, however, the violence in *Juice* was a means to an end. The film is about gaining respect in the community. In a scene before the robbery that changes their lives forever, Bishop states, "We run from the cops. . . . We run from security guards. . . . Feel like I'm on the damn track team." To which Q replies, "If you want respect, you gotta earn it." Bishop then responds, "You gotta be ready to throw down. Stand up and die for that stuff, if you want some juice." Filmmaker Ernest Dickerson seemed to be suggesting that when young men commit violent offenses, they gain respect in their community. He did not, however, explore the reason(s) that the youths in *Juice* equated criminal activity with respect. Generally, participants criticized the aesthetic construction of the film because they had difficulty understanding the reason for the violence. They blamed their lack of understanding on the director's inability to adequately tell the story of the four young men.

In contrast, the violence in *Boyz n the Hood* appeared to be a normal part of everyday life. Its purpose was to establish order in the community, which was to a large extent enforced by various gangs. That is why Doughboy's gang seeks revenge on the rival gang members who killed his brother Ricky. In this society, the punishment for murder is murder. The separateness of the community from the larger society resulted in a "war zone," represented by the police helicopter lights and gunfire that Brandi sees and hears while doing her homework. The surveillance from up above represents the attitude of the police on managing the black population confined within this particular area of the city. And when cops are present on the street, they also behave in violent ways. In the scene in which Tre and Ricky are driving home, they are stopped by Officer Coffey and his partner. Officer Coffey, a black patrolman, is the one who puts a gun to Tre's head while spouting words that reflect the hatred that he feels for those who he believes make it difficult for others in the race. Coffey represents the acculturation of racist ideology as it exists within American society by one who resides in the marginalized group that he so despises. Several participants articulated how "moved" or sad they felt that people lived that way—that they must be subjected to such humiliation. In that sense, they appeared to have been drawn into the "realistic" representation of the violence in the film because of the plausibility of the story. And although the violence in the film is also stylized (e.g., when Ricky is shot it was also in slow motion, with only the sound of gunshots in the background), it is still not as graphic or as gritty as the violence depicted in Menace II Society. Unlike with Menace, participants were not shocked by the violence. Violence, as constructed in Boyz n the Hood, seemed quite natural.

Consequently, the critical orientation of group members ranged from sociological for Menace II Society to aesthetic criticism for Juice to psychosocial for Boyz n the Hood. The features of the texts that best account for the differences in the participants' responses can be attributed to the representation of mainstream American society. In Menace II Society, after the opening sequence in the convenience store, the scene shifts to dramatic black-and-white footage of the race riots in Watts, California. Through voice-over, Caine states, "After the riots, the drugs started." The scene then shifts to a party at Caine's childhood home, where his mother is high on drugs and his father shoots a man to death. In effect, filmmakers Allen and Albert Hughes seem to be suggesting that mainstream society was to blame for the conditions that existed in the hood. The use of footage from an actual occurrence also helps to link the film to the larger society—placing its events within a historical context. In this way, they provided a sociological reason for Caine's behavior that was linked, in fact, to reality.

In contrast, the director of Juice did not suggest that the behavior of the characters was a part of a larger social problem (i.e., racism). Instead, he attributed Bishop's behavior to some intrapersonal problem in that there is no explicit reason given for his violent and erratic behavior. Bishop lives in an apartment in Harlem with his family. He does not appear to be particularly isolated or unloved. He has a grandmother and a father. Nor does he seem to act out of the norm during the first part of the film. Bishop's activities appear to involve typical teenage engagements, such as skipping school and hanging out with friends. Therefore, it is most likely that many participants were uncomfortable linking his behavior to mental illness because it is not adequately supported by the narrative. Additionally, the filmmaker may not have satisfied participants' expectations for the genre. *Juice* was the only film shown in class in which the behavior of the characters was not attributed to mainstream society (a common theme in hood films). The need to attribute violence to the larger society provides the participant with the distance he or she needs to see the good in troubled characters. They would like to see that their circumstances are not solely of their own making—that there are larger forces at play. Thus, participants discussed the aesthetic construction of *Juice* in an attempt to determine what would make the characters in the film more believable. In looking for the redemptive value of the characters, they ultimately expressed their desire to see more multidimensional, young black males who are just friends—a narrative absent of criminal activity.

Like *Menace*, the narrative of *Boyz n the Hood* also linked the problems in the community to the larger society. In the opening scene of *Boyz*, viewers are given statistics on black-on-black crime. About halfway through the film, Furious Styles delivers a lecture on the negative consequences of gentrification for people living in black American communities. Under a sign that offers cash for homes, Furious tells the group that has assembled that they need to keep the community black, with black-owned businesses. When an elderly gentleman tells him that the people in the community are the ones killing themselves with crack cocaine, Furious tells the crowd that black people are not the ones who bring drugs into the country and into the neighborhood. He states, "We don't own any planes. We don't own no ships. We're not the people flyin' or floatin' that shit in here." He goes on to talk about the number of liquor stores and gun shops in the neighborhood. When the same elderly gentleman asks why, Furious states, "Because they want us to kill ourselves. You go out to Beverly Hills you don't see that shit." "They," of course, refers to those in power, that is, the dominant culture. In the final scene of the film, Doughboy painfully talks about being disconnected from mainstream American society. The morning after avenging the death of his brother, Doughboy tells Tre, "Turned on the TV this morning. They had all this shit on about livin' in a violent, violent world. Showed all these foreign places—where foreigners live, and all. Started thinkin', man. Either they don't know, or don't show, or don't care about what's going on in the hood. They had all this foreign shit. They didn't have shit on my brother." In contrast to Menace II Society, Boyz n the Hood examined racism from an individual, contemporary viewpoint instead of situating it in history and representing its long-lasting effects on a community. In this way, Boyz elicited a psychosocial analysis from participants. Generally, the responses to all three films indicate that the participants' critical orientation was based on the directors' view of the hood, except when that view was not clearly articulated and failed to meet the participants' expectations for the genre, as in the case of Juice.

Over the course of the three discussions, participants maintained a consistent aesthetic distance from each film. Their responses to the hood films shown in class were "warm" in that the topics addressed in the films seemed important to the members of the group. However, the reasons for the emotional tone of their responses varied from film to film. While discussing Menace II Society, participants seemed very concerned with the impact of the film on its audience. When engaged in dialogue about Juice, they ridiculed the film because it did not meet the standards for "good" filmmaking. During the discussion of Boyz n the Hood, participants expressed how "moved" they were by the film because it was a sad commentary on American society. It appeared that the genre elicited a "warm" response because it examined problems that have an impact on American society as a whole. Since participants often discussed the films in terms of their "realism," the representation of the social and physical space that the characters occupied in hood films seemed to best account for the consistency in the emotional tone of their responses.

The Role of the Reader in Shaping Response

The narrative construction of the films, which focused on the lives of young African American males in urban environments, seemed to encourage participants to use their own experiences and background to make meaning. Not surprisingly, many of the students discussed the films in terms of their own life experiences, ethnic or racial group identification, gender, and socioeconomic class membership. Some participants raised topics that reflected their own backgrounds, particularly when accessing "realism." Samantha, for example, was concerned with the representation of Latinos in *Menace II Society*. Several participants talked about their life experiences as a means to support their statements. Most notably, during the discussion of *Menace II Society*, Tracie mentioned that even though she is white and middle class, she understands that racism exists because she has a black boyfriend. During the discussion of *Juice*, Donna commented that she could understand Q dating an older woman because she had dated a younger man. Therefore, it appeared that participants commented on scenes that had some relevance to their own personal lives. However, while the characteristics of the reader helped shape the focus of participants' attention, it did not play a major role during the discussions.

Similarly, the critical orientation of the group's members was influenced by their socioeconomic class. Many of the participants felt the need to distance themselves educationally and economically from the perceived target audience for the films. For instance, Brenda routinely mentioned how she would not interpret a film the same as nonpresent "others" because of the educational level that she had attained. In a sense, participants believed that they had acquired knowledge that allowed them to interpret the films in a particular way. Since they generally saw themselves as separate from the audience for hood films, their approach to analyzing the films generally adhered to formal schools of thought that address questions of human behavior (i.e., psychology and sociology) and film theory.

Memories of past viewing experiences also played a small role in shaping participants' critical orientation. Clearly, participants held specific expectations for each hood film because they compared and contrasted them to other films both inside and outside the genre. During the discussion of *Juice*, their knowledge of cinematic conventions did not allow them to address issues directly related to human behavior (i.e., sociology and psychology) because the film did not meet their expectations for hood films and films in general. In contrast, *Boyz n the Hood* and *Menace II Society* were analyzed from a sociological and psychological perspective because they were perceived to be more "realistic."

Each participant's aesthetic distance from the texts was significantly influenced by his or her personal characteristics and experiences. For example, some participants made reference to their ethnic or racial group as a means to define themselves for the other members, to defend a position, and/or to justify the way that they felt. On one occasion, David attempted to explain his interest in the genre when he said, "These films talk to me, and I'm a middle-class white kid." His statement seems to suggest that one does not have to be black and lower class to be able to relate to hood films. This statement is significant in that it not only justified his position within the group but also begins to explain the attraction of ghettocentric or hood films for nonblacks with seemingly no physical or social proximity to the hood. In another instance, while talking about *Menace II Society*, Erika stated that as a black woman, she was offended by a statement that Brenda made about black men dating white women. Brenda's remark sparked a very heated debate on interracial dating. Overall, it appeared that the discussions that surrounded references to the personal characteristics and experiences of participants were, at a minimum, "warm."

Similarly, the emotional tone of participants' responses intensified when they discussed their life experiences. It appeared that the ability (or inability) to experientially connect to the characters in the films made participants more (or less) involved in the narrative content of a particular film. In effect, their experiences seemed to increase or decrease the emotional tone of their responses. For instance, Greg made it clear that he could only indirectly relate to the specifics of *Juice*. During the discussion of *Boyz n the Hood*, Greg commented that he highly doubted that he would drive or walk through Compton or Crenshaw; therefore, his only exposure to ghetto life is through these films. Correspondingly, his emotional tone throughout the discussions was generally "cool." Participants who talked about more direct experiences with the kinds of people represented in hood films had "warmer" responses. When Mark mentioned that *Menace II Society* was better than *Boyz n the Hood*, his tone was "warm," as he stated, "In other films, in other life situations, I've seen people who have no real sense of hope." It therefore seemed that personal life experiences and statements of identity elicit strong feelings because they reveal a part of a participant's character. In this way, the characteristics/experiences of the reader play a major role in determining a participant's aesthetic distance from the texts.

The Role of the Immediate
Social Context in Shaping Response

During the discussions of *Menace II Society* and *Juice*, the first person to raise a topic helped determine where participants focused their attention. For example, Donna was the first person to respond during the discussion of *Menace II Society*. In raising the topic of the audience, she helped direct participants' attention to the world outside the film. While discussing *Boyz n the Hood*, however, the second person to raise a topic focused the attention of the group. My increased participation in the discussion suggests that participants had exhausted some of the topics common to hood films in the first two discussions (e.g., experiential connection, realism, and so on) and were searching for new ideas.

Generally, topics were maintained throughout a discussion because participants incorporated the previous comment into their own response before introducing a new subject. When one member raised a topic that was ignored or not supported by another member of the group, the topic died out. Generally, that participant did not raise the topic again. For example, Samantha's comment on the representation of Latinos in *Menace II Society* did not receive a verbal response from her non-Hispanic classmates. As a result, the issue was not debated. This strongly suggests that the interaction of culturally diverse others had a significant effect on the direction in which participants focused their attention.

When a participant raised a topic that led to a dispute, he or she either intensified or modified his or her talk, accepted the other participant's statements, or withdrew from the conversation. Generally, as participants discussed *Menace II Society* and *Juice*, they intensified their responses in the face of actual or anticipated rebuttal. It is important to note, however, that when discussing *Juice*, they were less emotionally and experientially connected to the film's narrative than to the other films. Therefore, the discussion was less personal, and participants could intensify their statements without potentially offending anyone. During the discussion of *Boyz n the Hood*, they seemed to accept the positions of the other participants. This sequence suggests that participants learned from the discussion on *Menace II Society*, in which a topic became too "hot," in that information after a point was no longer being processed. Strong emotional energy was expended, but no resolution was reached. As a result, participants adjusted their understanding of the group by avoiding potentially controversial topics (e.g., racism, the marginalization of women, and the representation of others).

The critical orientation of the group was decided early on in the discussions. Generally, the first few comments set the path for the participants to follow. While other forms of analysis surfaced throughout the course of each discussion, the critical orientation remained relatively consistent. Participants' responses to one another contributed to the original position. However, as mentioned earlier, the critical orientation was best accounted for by the features of the texts because participants essentially followed the path set by the directors of the films.

Generally, participants' responses to one another had somewhat of an impact on their aesthetic distance from the texts. Although it appeared that supporting statements by others did not intensify the emotional tone of the conversation, conflicting statements almost always increased the emotional tone of the response because participants often relied on their personal experiences to make their point.

Generalizations

Based on my analysis of the group discussions, the text, the personal characteristics and life experiences of the reader, and the immediate social context all played important roles in shaping participants' meaning-making responses.

The direction in which participants focused their attention was most significantly shaped by the features of the text and the immediate social context. The representation of violence in hood films and the participants' interactions with "others" shaped the topics that were discussed. Similarly, the critical orientation of group members was also best accounted for by the features of the text. An analysis of the representation of mainstream American society in each film suggests that participants followed the critical orientation of the filmmaker when his view was clearly articulated and when the participants' expectations for the genre had been met. Finally, a participant's aesthetic distance from the text was most significantly shaped by the personal characteristics and life experiences of the reader and to a lesser extent by the immediate social context. Participants made reference to their race, gender, socioeconomic status, and life experiences as a means to position themselves in relationship to the texts. Their interaction with other group members influenced the emotional intensity with which they negotiated conflicting viewpoints.

~

CHAPTER SIX

Epilogue

The representation of young, black urban males in ghettocentric street films has been the focus of widespread social concern and debate since the early 1990s. The genre has generated a great deal of interest because of its depiction of the economic and social disparity present in American society from the point of view of the disenfranchised—a voice seldom heard in mainstream Hollywood cinema. Adding to the controversy are several outbreaks of violence that occurred throughout the country at the time of these films' theatrical releases that called attention to the impact of the genre on its audience. In an attempt to give meaning to the films and those incidents, many cultural critics, theater executives, and filmmakers have commented on the racialized responses of black and white audiences to the genre, thus defining black males as the producers, consumers, and perpetrators of violent activity. I, however, am interested in how viewers' responses to a particular cinematic construction of "blackness" are shaped by their immediate social context. In other words, I am suggesting that meaning can also be constructed, at least in some cases, during its expression to specific others in dialogue and that the dynamics of the dialogue and the relations among the participants play a major role in the meanings readers give to texts. Specifically, I am concerned with the notion of meaning making within the context of a multicultural setting when the readers are young adults responding to a particular construction of "blackness" as represented in the hood films *Menace II Society*, *Juice*, and *Boyz n the Hood*.

The response of critics and the reaction of audiences to the films at the time of their theatrical release highlighted the questions of this study—that is, questions about the roles played in audiences' meaning making and response by the "messages" in "the text itself," the experiences audiences bring to the text, the sociocultural "situation" of different audiences, and the immediate social context in which meanings and responses are constructed.

Overview

In this study, I analyzed the meaning-making responses of an ethnically diverse group of coeducational college students to hood films. The purpose of the study was to examine how the films themselves, unique characteristics that viewers bring to the films, and the immediate social context and the dynamics of response shape meaning making. All fourteen participants who enrolled in a course (that I instructed) on African American cinema at a major university consented to having their responses to *Menace II Society*, *Juice*, and *Boyz n the Hood* analyzed for the purposes of this research. The procedures followed in the study were part of the normal teaching methods for the course.

At the beginning of the semester, I informed students that their discussions would be audiotaped to help me in planning future class lessons. Throughout the course of the semester, students viewed and discussed (with low teacher involvement) each of the scheduled films on the syllabus. After each era in contemporary black cinema (i.e., blaxploitation, the L.A. Rebellion, and the hood) was discussed, students wrote a three-page response to a film or films of their choosing for that particular era. At the end of the semester, after they had received their grades for the course, they were informed that I would like to further study their verbal responses to the hood films that we discussed in class and for which they wrote a paper. Further, students interested in allowing their oral responses to be included in the study were instructed to return the consent form and background questionnaire to me in a sealed envelope.

After obtaining information on each participant from the background questionnaire, a profile of the population under study was constructed. Generally, all the students in the class met the requirements for middle-class membership. They ranged in age from nineteen to twenty-nine, with an average age of twenty-two. There were ten women and four men in the class. Several ethnic groups were represented: African American, European (or Caucasian) American, Asian, Asian American, Hispanic, and racially or ethnically mixed. African (or black) American females made up the largest group in the class.

The research involved an analysis of the dynamics of the group discussions following the class's viewing of three hood films. My central concern was the nature of participation, the establishing or changing of topics, points of conflict, and the themes that characterized the discussions for each film. Each group discussion was also summarized with respect to its focus of attention, critical orientation, aesthetic distance, and conflict management and resolution strategies. The purpose of this analysis was primarily to examine the role of the different texts in shaping response, to illuminate the oral response strategies used by students in a multicultural classroom, and to examine the ways in which the dynamics of the participants' interactions with each other shaped the meanings articulated.

The Representation of Violence and the Immediate Social Context

The dialogue during the group discussions was a clear indication that the nature of urban youth films and the immediate social context in which they are shown and discussed played a significant role in the meanings that were derived. Together, they had the greatest impact on what participants talked about during the discussion and how they responded in the presence of culturally diverse others. Violence as perpetrated by young black males is a significant and inextricable part of hood films of the 1990s. Therefore, it is not surprising that participants focused their attention on that aspect of the films. The films are about black males coming of age in a society in which to be a "man" they must learn to defend themselves in an environment that has been neglected by the larger society. They live in a place where the majority of the male residents equate respect with a gun. Because violence is normalized and contained within the community, it devastates the community—perpetuating more violence.

Although it is clear why the representation of violence was the most important aspect of the films for participants, within the group setting it appeared that certain topics were not addressed because of the ethnic/racial composition of the group. And while some of the topics raised were not addressed, other topics were avoided. In a sense, the fear of negative responses (articulated and in the mind of participants) from other group members may have caused participants to focus their attention on a particular topic in order shift the focus away from more sensitive topics. In other words, it appeared that participants may not have focused their attention on certain topics so completely (for example, the discussion of the audience for *Menace*) if they shared the same cultural/ethnic background.

In addition, there were very few discussions on the representation of women in the films—which was somewhat surprising given the composition of the group and the negative ways in which women were depicted. I can only surmise that because the films so heavily emphasize the impact of violence and poverty on black male youth, black women are not the focus of the narrative and therefore not the focus of the discussion. I would also argue, however, that the women in the group (specifically the black women) were much more concerned with issues pertaining to race than with gender when discussing the representation of underclass black communities in a multicultural setting—highlighting what was of greatest importance in that particular place and time.

Critical Orientation and the Representation of Mainstream American Society

The relative position or role that participants assumed in responding to the film was most determined by the films themselves. The construction of American society in hood films had a definite impact on what knowledge (sociological, psychological, aesthetic, and so on) participants brought to bear in their interpretation of the narrative. They seemed to follow the critical orientation of the filmmaker when the expectations for the genre had been met. In general, mainstream society as represented in hood films is not in most cases visibly present on the screen. In many films, however, it is to blame for the conditions that exist in the hood.

Readers, Context, and Aesthetic Distance

Overall, the participants' aesthetic distance to the texts seemed to be the most affected by the characteristics/experiences of the reader and to a lesser extent the immediate social context. The emotional tone of their responses were directly related to the articulation of personal life experiences, background information, and feelings. The more a participant discussed his or her life experiences, background, and feelings, the more his or her emotional tone increased. In revealing their life experiences to other members in the group, participants made themselves vulnerable to the reactions of other group members—which was reflected in the emotional tone of their talk. Participants' aesthetic distance from the text was also shaped by the immediate social context, particularly when they were engaged in conflicts that involved references to personal characteristics and experiences.

As a black woman teaching a course on black cinema, it is more than possible that my appearance as well as my teaching style (which included the use of self-managed group discussions) may have encouraged some participants to express themselves more strongly on issues of race and gender than they might in discussing these issues with someone of a different age, gender, or ethnic background in my presence. Participants may have found it easier to express themselves to me, in general, because of my perceived perspective on the texts. In other words, they accessed the social space that I occupy and as a result found some level of comfort in articulating more controversial issues—which strongly suggests that response is to a large extent dependent on its audience. Some evidence of this was also found in student writings on the topic of hood films. Although not systematically explored in this study (but certainly worthy of future research), several participants who identified themselves as at least part black wrote extremely passionate papers examining one or more of the films. Donna, for instance, in the first paragraph of her paper, wrote,

> Since these films cinematically reveal the sociological and psychological positioning of a people, one has no choice but to accept these messages as evidence of relations between black males and females. Also all the films are about the plight of black males as if women's suffering is not as meaningful nor as storyworthy. . . . Perhaps it is not the fault of [black] people due to the intense psychological beating at the hands of the white power structure.

The emotional tone of Donna's paper appeared antagonistic in that she often used words that were accusatory, contemptuous, and inflammatory. She wrote, "*Juice* blatantly displays the lack of respect and the demeaning treatment extended from male to female." She went on to write that "in the movie [*Boyz n the Hood*], the infamous 'bitch' word jumps off the screen to bite the enlightened black female in the butt." Her colorful descriptors and the frequency with which they were used provide some insight into the passion that Donna felt toward the subject matter, thereby suggesting a high level of emotional attachment or a "very hot" response. This is particularly important given the general assumption that the written text is a cooler medium than verbal responses in a group setting. Donna, Mark, and Brenda all seemed to express a stronger emotional tone in writing than in the group discussions. This also suggests that some participants may have been hesitant to make provocative statements in the group setting because of the anticipated reactions of others. Specifically, participants may not have wanted to offend another member of the group or create any additional conflicts among group members, as Donna, Mark, and Brenda articulated strong emotional feelings about white, mainstream culture. Those participants, at least, felt comfortable in increasing the emotional tone of their statements to me in writing.

Implications for Reader-Response Theory

The findings of this study suggest that participants were affected by the immediate social context. Therefore, it lends support to the context-centered theory of reader-response criticism as put forth by Janet Staiger, which suggests that meaning is not solely a response to a text, to the reader's own experiences, or to the context of setting and institutions but is a negotiation among all those factors.[1] Thus, there is no "real" response that is more "authentic" than others in that all responses are conditioned to some extent by their immediate social context.

Moreover, the findings call into question the rigidness of the text-centered approach, whose proponents assume that the text is always decoded in the manner in which it was encoded. Adherents of that theory assume that meaning is the product of the author. During the discussion of *Menace II Society*, however, participants thought that everyone died at the end of the film except O-Dog—when, in fact, Stacey also lived. As a result, their conversation was affected by their "misinterpretation" of the text.

In addition, this study provides questions for some adherents of the reader-centered approach who contend that a response is solely the "product" of the individual—the result of his or her background. While the reader's background plays an important role in determining his or her response, meaning is also contingent on an individual's relationship to others. Meanings in the group discussions were dynamically negoti- ated in that various participants set the topics for the discussion, chose to participate or not participate in the circulation of ideas, debated, and listened to the responses of others while making the necessary adjust- ments to their understanding of the text. Moreover, meaning was con- tingent on the participants' assumptions about me as a teacher and as a person. Therefore, response is the product not only of the individual but also of the space that he or she occupies in a particular context of interactions with others.

This study also suggests that participants were aware of the readings that "others" give to texts. In the first discussion, participants articu- lated what they perceived to be the responses of less educated and/or nonblack audiences to the film. This seemed to suggest that viewers were aware that readers of different socioeconomic and ethnic/racial groups interpret hood films differently. Therefore, it supports Hall's en- coding/decoding model of communication in that the articulated change in participants' responses as they compared their past viewing

experiences to their readings of the films in class suggests that as college students they have learned to negotiate their readings of hood
films.[2] Generally, participants' responses changed in relationship to the
films because their knowledge increased about the environment represented in the film. In this regard, they reworked the narrative in order
to take into account the social differences of different responders. This
lends support to the idea that multicultural groups in shared response
alter public space in ways in which ethnic and/or racially homogeneous
groups do not.

Pedagogical Implications

Since the viewing experiences described in this study took place in a
college classroom, I feel that it is important to include some implications for teachers who use film as an instructional tool. The first issue
involves the use of "controversial" (or hot-button) material. During
group discussions, when a topic became too "hot," such as on the topic
of interracial dating (as in the talk surrounding *Menace II Society*), participants no longer appeared to listen to the other members in the
group. The discussion sparked a debate that appeared to leave participants feeling hurt and unsatisfied, while some other scenes in the film
that represented interracial conflict were not addressed—specifically
the opening sequence in the convenience store in *Menace II Society* in
which O-Dog shot a Korean shopkeeper. Therefore, self-managed
groups may not be the most effective way of talking about sensitive issues in culturally diverse settings. More moderator involvement would
probably help participants discuss issues without losing sight of the purpose of the conversation, that is, to gain understanding. Therefore, I
believe that it would be useful for teachers to identify potential "hot"
topics in advance so that they are able to guide the discussion in a way
that elicits responses about other important issues in the films as well
as bringing out responses from participants who are not as emotionally
charged. In that way, participants can engage in a more productive dialogue about important issues.

Specifically, for teachers of film, it is important to engage in discussing the aesthetic construction of films more fully than these participants did. In this study, participants were more aesthetically critical of

the film they did not like. However, the same critique should have been applied to all the films under discussion. In talking about films that represent "reality," teachers might start the conversation by discussing the techniques that the filmmaker used to evoke certain responses, such as lighting, camera angle, composition, and so on, before moving into a discussion on the narrative content and/or the audience for the film. In that way, students may have a more well-rounded discussion.

Further, one of the major concerns that I had with the discussions of the films was that participants generally did not discuss material from the course's text. Only one student (Robert) explicitly talked about the assigned reading. Based on their verbalization of material from the text during the discussions of other films in the class that were not part of the hood genre (i.e., blaxploitation and the L.A. Rebellion), it seemed that participants were more experientially and emotionally connected to ghettocentric youth films and therefore relied more heavily on their own interpretation of the film than that of an "authority" figure. For that reason, it would be useful for teachers of film to ask students about the text and how it relates to their own views on the film. In that way, students would be encouraged to deconstruct the arguments of "experts"—a practice that is, in my experience, uncommon in undergraduate classrooms.

Moreover, ghettocentric youth films deal with some of the most frightening issues in America: racism, sexism, hopelessness, violence, and isolation. In this regard, hood films could elicit different meaning-making processes than other genres. For instance, participants may engage in warmer, more personalized conversations when talking about hood films than a film in another genre. As a teacher, this genre was particularly difficult to deal with because participants in a culturally diverse classroom seemed reluctant to discuss certain issues for fear of accidentally offending someone. Therefore, it would be important to keep students focused on the specifics of the texts by directing them to the assigned reading when the discussions become too personal. Participants could be encouraged to engage the author of the assigned reading in debate. In that way, they could distance themselves somewhat from the films themselves. The purpose of this is not to negate the importance of life experiences but to allow other voices to be heard.

The Genre

Earlier it was suggested that the theatrical showing of hood films could have had an impact on the violent outbreaks that accompanied some of the screenings in theaters across the country. Although the responses of college students in a classroom setting do not replicate the social context of a theater, the findings suggest that films in the genre can elicit "warm" responses from viewers. Clearly, images of black males when constructed as ghettocentric and thereby embodying the negative features of the hood elicit strong responses. Participants expressed deep emotional and experiential connections to the themes addressed in the film. The images seemed to tap into the cultural fears, anger, and hopelessness of the audience. Hence, it could be suggested that the social context of meaning making—specifically an interactive, intercultural dialogue, such as discussed here—is a significant moment in this process. This is just as, if not more, important than the physical context (a darkened theater). As this study supports, meaning is constructed not in isolation but rather through the interplay of individuals, texts, and their cultural contexts.

Notes

1. Janet Staiger, *Interpreting Films* (Princeton, NJ: Princeton University Press, 1992).
2. Stuart Hall, "Encoding/Decoding," in *Culture, Media, Language*, ed. Stuart Hall, Dorothy Hobson, Andrew Lowe, and Paul Willis (London: Hutchinson, 1980), 128–38.

Appendix A: Course Films

The course on contemporary black cinema emphasized semiotic, sociological, and historical models of representation in black American film from the 1970s to the 1990s. Three interrelated cycles were explored—blaxploitation, the L.A. Rebellion, and hood films. One of the purposes of the course was to provoke discussion on the politics of representation in American society. Following are my impressions of student responses from all the films shown during the course of the semester. They are presented here only to offer some insight into other class discussions—as a way to provide a larger context for the films under study. With the exception of *Menace II Society*, *Juice*, and *Boyz n the Hood*, responses were not analyzed in any systematic way.

Sweet Sweetback's Baadasssss Song (1971)
Director: Melvin Van Peebles
Screenplay: Melvin Van Peebles
Cast: Melvin Van Peebles (Sweetback), Simon Chuckster (Beetle), John Dullaghan (Commissioner), West Gale, Hubert Scales (Mu-Mu)

After saving a young revolutionary from police brutality, Sweetback is on the run for his life. The film takes the viewer on his journey as he eludes capture, aided by "the black community." The film has several graphic sex scenes. Therefore, before showing it, I prepared students by telling them what to expect. After screening the film, they seemed somewhat hesitant to respond. I asked them several questions about the main character, Sweetback, and his role in the film. Most of the students were quiet throughout the discussion. With some coaxing, however, they were soon able to discuss the significance of the character as well as the filmmaker's technique. A couple of students referred to the main text explicitly as they discussed how a film with such a strong political statement got made.

Shaft (1971)
Director: Gordon Parks
Screenplay: Ernest Tidyman and John D. F. Black
Novel: Ernest Tidyman
Cast: Richard Roundtree (John Shaft), Moses Gunn (Bumpy Jonas), Charles Cioffi (Vic Androzzi), Christopher St. John (Ben Buford), Gwenn Mitchell (Ellie Moore), Lawrence Pressman (Sergeant Tom Hannon)

Students appeared to be very interested in the film's narrative about a black detective who negotiates between the black and white worlds of New York City. The focus of the discussion was on what Shaft represented. Students thought that his actions and his appearance signified confidence or sexual prowess (i.e., black macho). A couple of the students referred to the main text for the course to talk about the novel on which the film was based and the decision to cast the role of Shaft with a black actor. They seemed to enjoy talking about his character and why it is still part of popular culture today.

Superfly (1972)
Director: Gordon Parks Jr.
Screenplay: Phillip Fenty
Cast: Ron O'Neal (Youngblood Priest), Carl Lee (Eddie), Sheila Frazier (Georgia), Julius Harris (Scatter), Charles MacGregor (Fat Freddy)

The film is about Youngblood Priest, a cocaine dealer trying to leave a life of crime, and the obstacles he faces from those whose benefit it is for him to stay in. During the discussion, students spent a significant amount of time talking about how "whiteness" and "blackness" are represented in the film. For instance, they seemed quite interested in comparing Priest's relationship with his white girlfriend to that with his black girlfriend. They were also very interested in the religious symbols that surrounded Priest—his name, an angel as a car ornament, and so on. It was a very active discussion.

Black Shadows on a Silver Screen (1975)
Director: Ray Hubbard
Writing Credit: Thomas Cripps
   The purpose of the documentary was to provide students with a brief history of blacks in film before discussing the contemporary films that were the focus of the course. Students generally just responded to questions that I asked.

She's Gotta Have It (1986)
Director: Spike Lee
Screenplay: Spike Lee
Cast: Tracy Camilla Johns (Nola Darling), Tommy Raymond Hicks (Jamie Overstreet), John Canada Terrell (Greer Childs), Spike Lee (Mars Blackmon), Raye Dowell (Opal Gilstrap), Joie Lee (Clorinda Bradford)
   She's Gotta Have It is about a sexually liberated woman who dates three men at the same time— all with distinct personalities. I began the discussion asking students what the film was about. Someone gave me a general summary. The question then arose about whose story was actually being told. I reminded students about one of the major criticisms of the film (from an article they had read) regarding what some scholars see as a negative representation of women in the film. Many of the women said that they understood how the film could be interpreted in that way. Since the majority of the film was in black and white, I also asked students to tell me about the only scene in the film that was in color. Overall, this was a very active discussion. (Although Spike Lee is not a part of the L.A. Rebellion in that he is the product of New York University's film school, he is included in this course because of his importance to black independent cinema.)

To Sleep with Anger (1990)
Director: Charles Burnett
Screenplay: Charles Burnett
Cast: Danny Glover (Harry), Paul Butler (Gideon), Mary Alice (Suzie), Carl Lumbly (Junior), Vonetta McGee (Pat), Sheryl Lee Ralph (Linda), Richard Brooks (Babe Brother), Ethel Ayler (Hattie), Julius Harris (Herman), Sy Richardson (Slash), Davis Roberts (Okra Tate)

To Sleep with Anger is about a southern drifter named Harry who surfaces at the Los Angeles home of a family he knew many years before. To start the discussion, I asked students to tell me what the film was about. They talked about the conflicts that existed within the film, such as the struggle between the past and the present and good and evil. They also talked about Harry's role in the film and the representation of mainstream society. The more they talked, the more they seemed to appreciate the symbolic nature of the film.

Daughters of the Dust (1991)
Director: Julie Dash
Screenplay: Julie Dash
Cast: Cora Lee Day (Nana Peazant), Alva Rogers (Eula Peazant), Barbara O. Jones (Yellow Mary), Trula Hoosier (Trula), Umar Abdurrahamn (Bilal Muhammad), Adisa Anderson (Eli Peazant), Bahni Turpin (Iona Peazant), Cheryl Lynn Bruce (Viola Peazant), Tommy Redmond Hicks (Mr. Snead)

Daughters of the Dust is about the migration of members of the Peazant family from one of the South Sea islands (off the coast of Georgia and South Carolina) to the mainland at the turn of the century and the potential loss of one's culture. During the screening, several students appeared to fidget. I addressed the issue directly by asking them what was going on. The unhurried pace of the film seemed to be the major cause of their discomfort. Students stated that they had grown accustomed to fast cuts in which a large amount of information is presented in a short amount of time. I then had them focus on the cinematography and how that helped to tell the story as well as focusing on the time in which the film was set. Near the end of the discussion, I informed them about the controversy surrounding the film regarding the use of Gullah dialect—which some critics argued makes it difficult to understand. Generally, they said that they appreciated the filmmaker staying true to the period. Student interest in the film seemed to slowly increase as they began to pose questions on their own.

Boyz n the Hood (1991)
Director: John Singleton
Screenplay: John Singleton
Cast: Ice Cube (Darin "Doughboy" Baker), Morris Chestnut (Rickey Baker), Cuba Gooding Jr. (Tre Styles), Lawrence Fishburne (Jason "Furious" Styles), Nia Long (Brandi), Angela Bassett (Reva Devereaux)

During the discussion of *Boyz n the Hood*, students discussed the "realistic" qualities of the film, their emotional feelings, the aesthetic construction of the film, the director, the theme of the film, the behavior of the characters, the film's audience, the message of the film, their personal backgrounds, and the controversy surrounding the advertising of hood films. They spent much of their time discussing the film's narrative and expressed strong emotions relative to the plight of the characters.

Juice (1992)
Director: Ernest Dickerson
Screenplay: Ernest Dickerson and Gerard Brown
Cast: Tupac Shakur (Bishop), Khalil Kain (Raheem), Jermaine Hopkins (Steel), Omar Epps (Q), Cindy Herron (Yolanda), Queen Latifah (Ruffhouse MC), Vincent Laresca (Radamest), Samuel L. Jackson (Trip), Dr. Dre (Contest Judge), Ed Lover (Contest Judge), Fab 5 Freddy (Himself)

During the discussion of *Juice*, students were interested in the aesthetic construction of the film as it relates to specific characters and scenes, realism, their personal experience, the audience for the film, and the modification of the script for the film.

Menace II Society (1993)
Directors: Allen and Albert Hughes
Screenplay: Allen Hughes, Albert Hughes, Tyger Williams
Cast: Tyrin Turner (Caine "Kaydee" Lawson), Larenz Tate (Kevin "O-Dog"), Glenn Plummer (Pernell), Jada Pinkett Smith (Ronnie), Vonte Sweet (Sharif), Charles S. Dutton (Mr. Butler), Samuel L. Jackson (Tat Lawson), Khandi Alexander (Kate Lawson)

When students discussed *Menace II Society*, they seemed most interested in the audience for the films, interracial dating, the film's message, realism, and the responsibility of the director. A major conflict occurred during a discussion regarding the representation of interracial dating. A large part of the discussion, however, focused on the audience for the film.

~

Appendix B: Additional Films

Over the past few years, the following films have been added to (or re-placed) films on the original syllabus. The comments that follow each film listed are my very general impressions of student talk and behavior based on teaching the same class at various institutions in a major met-ropolitan area. They are not the result of any systematic approach to the study of film.

Cotton Comes to Harlem (1970)
Director: Ossie Davis
Screenplay: Ossie Davis and Arnold Perl
Novel: Chester Himes
Cast: Godfrey Cambridge (Gravedigger Jones), Raymond St. Jacques (Coffin Ed Johnson), Calvin Lockhart (Reverend Deke O'Malley), Judy Pace (Iris), Redd Foxx (Uncle Bud), Emily Yancy (Mable), John Anderson (Bryce), Lou Jacobi (Goodman), Eugene Roche (Anderson), Cleavon Little (Lo Boy)

Police officers Gravedigger Jones and Coffin Ed Johnson are on the lookout for a bale of cotton that contains money that the Reverend Deke O'Malley has stolen from the people of Harlem under the guise of organizing a back-to-Africa trip. Students generally enjoy the film's narrative and are comfortable examining it from both a cultural and a historical perspective.

Killer of Sheep (1977)
Director: Charles Burnett
Screenplay: Charles Burnett
Cast: Henry Gayle Sanders (Stan), Kaycee Moore (Stan's Wife), Charles Bracy (Bracy), Angela Burnett (Stan's Daughter), Gene Cherry (Eugene), Jack Drummond (Stan's Son)

Filmed in black and white, *Killer of Sheep* is symbolic in its representation of the effects of poverty on a community. Generally, students initially experience some difficulty in associating various images with their meanings. The aesthetic construction of the film seems to require them to work harder to understand it than they are accustomed to doing. Generally, they have very little to say about the film without much prompting.

Ethnic Notions (1986)
Director: Marlon Riggs
Cast: Barbara T. Christian (Herself), Esther Rolle (Narrator)

This documentary historicizes stereotypical images of African Americans in film. Over the years, it seems that students in a multicultural setting appear to be less and less likely to want to discuss the issues raised by the film. Black students in class (depending on the number present) seem to ask more questions regarding what they have seen—relating their questions to the assigned reading from *Toms, Coons, Mulattos, Mammies, and Bucks* by Donald Bogle. Generally, when students are required to write a response paper to the documentary as a way to draw out additional responses, they seldom go beyond what is explicit on the screen.

Chameleon Street (1989)
Director: Wendell B. Harris Jr.
Screenplay: Wendell B. Harris Jr.
Cast: Wendell B. Harris Jr. (William Douglass Street), Angela Leslie (Gabrielle), Amina Fakir (Tatiana), Paula McGee (Herself), Richard David Kiley (Mr. Hand)

Based on a real person, the film follows William Douglass Street as he assumes different occupational roles (i.e., a Yale University student, a *Time* magazine reporter, a surgeon, and a lawyer) in society. The film is interesting in that there are many comedic moments in it (where students laugh outwardly) that do not seem very funny in the end. Students generally do not see the film as controversial at first, until the discussion, when they are asked to analyze the protagonist's behavior.

Do the Right Thing (1989)
Director: Spike Lee
Screenplay: Spike Lee
Cast: Danny Aiello (Sal), Ossie Davis (Da Mayor), Ruby Dee (Mother Sister), Richard Edson (Vito), Giancarlo Esposito (Buggin Out), Spike Lee (Mookie), Bill Nun (Radio Raheem), John Turturro (Pino), Paul Benjamin (ML)

I have shown this film in both introductory and more advanced film classes. Over the years, it has been (at various times) very disturbing for students. The representation/interaction of various ethnic/racial groups fuels the debate. One class in particular (that screened the film several years after its release) was rather upset that I had shown *Do the Right Thing* in class because it "stirs up racial problems." Other screenings of the film have been met with near silence. Both of these responses indicate that the issues raised by the film are still very important. They resonate with students—whether they can articulate their feelings or not. In these instances, I clearly point to the assigned reading for the film in order to provide some distance for the students.

One False Move (1992)
Director: Carl Franklin
Screenplay: Billy Bob Thornton, Tom Epperson
Cast: Bill Paxton (Chief Dale "Hurricane" Dixon), Cynda Williams (Lila "Fantasia" Walker), Billy Bob Thornton (Ray Malcolm), Michael Beach (Wade "Pluto" Franklin), Jim Metzler (Lt. Dudley "Dud" Cole)

After committing several murders, three criminals return to a small town where one of them grew up. The film is interesting in that it is one of only two films shown in class that does not have a predominantly black cast. During the discussion, students analyze the construction of the characters and their relationship to violence. But they seem most interested in the representation of blacks and whites and the representation of urban and rural environments.

Just Another Girl on the I.R.T. (1992)
Director: Leslie Harris
Screenplay: Leslie Harris
Cast: Ariyan A. Johnson (Chantel Mitchell), Kevin Thigpen (Tyrone), Ebony Jerido (Natete), Chequita Jackson (Paula), William Badget (Cedrick), Jerard Washington (Gerard), Tony Wilkes (Owen Mitchell), Karen Robinson (Debra Mitchell), Kisha Richardson (Lavonica), Monet Dunham (Denisha)

Set in Brooklyn, this is one of the few films written and directed by a woman. I show it because it offers a different perspective on the hood genre—where teenage pregnancy is more significant than black-on-black crime. Students seem to focus primarily on the film's narrative during the discussion. When prompted, they discuss the film's aesthetic construction.

Midnight Ramble: Oscar Micheaux and the History of Race Movies (1994)
Director: Pearl Bowser and Bestor Cram
Writing Credit: Clyde Taylor
Cast: Toni Cade Bambara, Robert Hall, Elton Fax, Pearl Bowser, Carlton Moss, Dorothy Delfs, Shingzie Howard, St. Claire Bourne Sr., Herb Jeffries, Edna Mae Harris, James Avery

In the beginning of the semester, students get a brief lecture on the early years of black filmmaking. This documentary helps them put contemporary filmmaking by African American filmmakers in perspective. Generally, students tend to treat the documentary strictly as a historical document from which they are rather distant. Many are preoccupied with taking notes. Usually, students just respond to the questions that I ask.

~

Appendix C:
Background Questionnaire

School: _____   Year: _____
                                        (Fr., Soph., Jr., Sr.)

Sex: _____ male   _____ female   Age: _____

Ethnicity: _____

1. In the past five years, did you permanently live with a parent or guardian?

   _____ a. yes   _____ b. no

The following section should be completed based on information from the head of household (parent, guardian, or self).

Family Information

2. What is the marital status of the head of household?

   _____ a. married   _____ c. widowed
   _____ b. single   _____ d. divorced

3. In the past five years, how many people have lived in your home, including yourself?

_____ a. 1   _____ d. 4   _____ g. 7   _____ more than 9
_____ b. 2   _____ e. 5   _____ h. 8
_____ c. 3   _____ f. 6   _____ i. 9

4. What is your family's total *gross* monthly household income?

_____ a. less than $500   _____ e. $2,001–$2,500

_____ b. $501–$1,000   _____ f. $2,501–$3,000

_____ c. $1,001–$1,500   _____ g. over $3,000

_____ d. $1,501–$2,000

5. What is the source of income for the head of household?

_____ a. job

_____ b. unemployment check

_____ c. benefit check (welfare)

_____ d. other, please specify _____

6. How many months has the person who serves as the head of household worked full-time in the past five years?

_____ a. less than 12 months   _____ d. 37–48 months

_____ b. 12–24 months   _____ e. 49–60 months

_____ c. 25–36 months

7. Please indicate the highest level of education for the person who serves as the head of household.

_____ a. no high school   _____ d. attended college

_____ b. some high school   _____ e. college graduate

_____ c. high school graduate/GED   _____ f. graduate school

8. Has anyone in your household, including yourself, ever served a prison term?

_____ a. yes   _____ b. no

If yes, please specify _____

9. Is there anyone in your household, including yourself, who is (or was) an unwed teenage parent?

_____ a. yes   _____ b. no

~

Bibliography

Althusser, Louis. *Ideology and Ideological State Apparatuses: Lenin and Philosophy and Other Essays.* London: New Left Books, 1971.

Angus, Ian, and Sut Jhally, eds. *Cultural Politics in Contemporary America.* New York: Routledge, 1989.

Antonio, Sheril D. *Contemporary African American Cinema.* New York: Peter Lang Publishing, 2002.

Austin, Regina. "'The Black Community,' Its Lawbreakers, and a Politics of Identification." *Southern California Law Review* 65, no. 4 (May 1992): 1769–1817.

Barthes, Roland. *Mythologies.* New York: Hill and Wang, 1972.

Bazin, Andre. *What Is Cinema?* Translated by Hugh Gray. 2 vols. Berkeley. University of California Press, 1967–1971.

Bell, Alan. "'Menace' Depicts Ghetto Life with Dead Accuracy." *Los Angeles Sentinel,* June 24, 1993, B-5.

Ben Chaim, Daphna. *Distance in the Theatre: The Aesthetics of Audience Response.* Ann Arbor, Mich.: UMI Research Press, 1984.

Berger, John. *Ways of Seeing.* Harmondsworth, Middlesex, England: Penguin, 1972.

Bezanson, Randall. "The 'Meaning' of First Amendment Speech." *ETC: A Review of General Semantics* 54 (1997): 133–49.

Bleich, David. "Epistomological Assumptions in the Study of Response." In *Reader-Response Criticism,* edited by Jane Tompkins, 134–63. Baltimore: The Johns Hopkins University Press, 1980. Originally published in 1978.

Bobo, Jacqueline. *Black Women as Cultural Readers.* New York: Columbia University Press, 1995.

Bogdan, Robert, and Sari Knopp Biklen. *Qualitative Research for Education*. 2nd ed. Boston: Allyn and Bacon, 1992.

Bogle, Donald. *Toms, Coons, Mullattoes, Mammies, and Bucks: An Interpretive History of Blacks in American Films*. 3rd ed. New York: Continuum Publishing, 1994.

Bordwell, David. *Making Meaning: Inference and Rhetoric in the Interpretation of Cinema*. Cambridge, Mass.: Harvard University Press, 1989.

Boyd, Todd. *Am I Black Enough for You? Popular Culture for the Hood and Beyond*. Bloomington: Indiana University Press, 1997.

Bradsher, Keith. "America's Opportunity Gap." *New York Times*, June 4, 1995, sec. 4, p. 4.

Bullough, Edward. "'Psychical Distance' as a Factor in Art and an Aesthetic Principle." *British Journal of Psychology* 5 (1912): 87–118.

Carbaugh, Donal. "Communication and Cultural Interpretation." *Quarterly Journal of Speech* 77 (1991): 336–42.

Carragee, Kevin M. "Interpretive Media Study and Interpretive Social Science." *Critical Studies in Mass Communication* 7 (1990): 81–96.

Cohen, Jeff. "The 'Relevance' of Cultural Identity in Audiences' Interpretations of Mass Media." *Critical Studies in Mass Communication* 8 (1991): 442–54.

Cripps, Thomas. *Black Film as Genre*. Bloomington: Indiana University Press, 1978.

Culler, Jonathan. "Literary Competence." In *Reader-Response Criticism*, edited by Jane Tompkins, 101–17. Baltimore: The Johns Hopkins University Press, 1980. Originally published in 1975.

Devine, Joel A., and James D. Wright. *The Greatest of Evils: Urban Poverty and the American Underclass*. New York: Aldine de Gruyter, 1993.

Diawara, Manthia, ed. *Black American Cinema*. New York: Routledge, 1993.

Dwyer, Victor. "Inner-City Heat," *Maclean's* 104, no. 30 (1991): 47.

Ebert, Roger. "Brilliant. *Boyz n the Hood* Combines Substance, Style." *Chicago Sunday Times*, July 12, 1991.

"The Education of Sonny Carson." *Ebony*, August 1974, 29: 157–59.

Ely, Margot, Maragaret Anzul, Teri Friedman, Diane Garner, and Ann McCormack Steinmetz. *Doing Qualitative Research: Circles within Circles*. New York: Falmer Press, 1991.

Entman, Robert M., and Andrew Rojecki. *The Black Image in the White Mind: Media and Race in America*. Chicago: University of Chicago Press, 2000.

Fish, Stanley. "Interpreting the Variorum." In *Reader-Response Criticism*, edited by Jane Tompkins, 164–84. Baltimore: The Johns Hopkins University Press, 1980. Originally published in 1976.

———. *Is There a Text in This Class? The Authority of Interpretive Communities*. London: Harvard University Press, 1982.

Fisher, Celeste. "'America's Worst Nightmare': Reading the Ghetto in a Culturally Diverse Context." In *Say It Loud! African-American Audiences, Media, and Identity*, edited by Robin R. Means-Coleman, 229–47. New York: Routledge, 2002.

Fisherkeller, Joellen. "Everyday Learning about Young Adolescents in Television Culture." *Anthropology and Education Quarterly* 28, no. 4 (1997): 467–93.

Fiske, John. *Television Culture*. London: Methune, 1987.

Fitzgerald, Thomas. "Media and Changing Metaphors of Ethnicity and Identity." *Media Culture and Society* 13 (1991): 193–214.

Fleming, Michael, and Jim Robbins. "H'wood Hangin with the 'Boyz.'" *Variety* 344, no. 2 (July 22, 1991): 1, 13.

Fox, David J., Scott Harris, and Jim Herron Zamora. "Nationwide Violence Mars Opening of 'Boyz' Movie." *Los Angeles Times*, July 14, 1991, A-1.

French, Mary Ann. "The Brothers Grim: Menace's Masterminds—Their 'Specialty' Is Violence." *Washington Post*, June 27, 1993, sec. G, p. 4.

Gates, Henry Lewis, Jr. "Literary Theory and the Black Tradition." In *Reception Study: From Literary Theory to Cultural Studies*, edited by James L. Machor and Philip Goldstein, 105–17. New York: Routledge, 2001.

George, Nelson. *Hip-Hop America*. New York: Penguin Books, 1999.

Glasgow, Douglas. *The Black Underclass: Poverty, Unemployment, and Entrapment of Ghetto Youth*. San Francisco: Jossey-Bass Publishers, 1980.

Grey, Herman. *Watching Race: Television and the Struggle for "Blackness."* Minneapolis: University of Minnesota Press, 1998.

Guerrero, Ed. *Framing Blackness: The African American Image in Film*. Philadelphia: Temple University Press, 1993.

Hall, Edward. *The Silent Language*. New York: Doubleday, 1981.

Hall, Stuart. "Encoding/Decoding." In *Culture, Media, Language*, edited by Stuart Hall, Dorothy Hobson, Andrew Lowe, and Paul Willis, 128–38. London: Hutchison, 1980.

Harris, Scott. "Mixed Reviews for Audience of Gang Movie." *Los Angeles Times*, June 17, 1993, B2.

Hawkins, Homer, and Richard Thomas. "White Policing of Black Populations: A History of Race and Social Control in America." In *Out of Order? Policing Black People*, edited by Ellis Cashmore and Eugene McLaughlin, 65–86. London: Routledge, 1991.

Heller, Celia S., ed. *Structured Social Inequality: A Reader in Comparative Social Stratification*. New York: Macmillan Publishing, 1987.

hooks, bell. "The Oppositional Gaze: Black Female Spectators." In *Black American Cinema*, edited by Manthia Diawara, 288–302. New York: Routledge, 1993.

———. *Yearning: Race, Gender, and Cultural Politics*. Boston: South End Press, 1990.

Iser, Wolfgang. "The Reading Process: A Phenomenological Approach." In *Reader-Response Criticism*, edited by Jane Tompkins, 50–69. Baltimore: The Johns Hopkins University Press, 1980.

Ittelson, William, and Hedley Cantril. *Perception: A Transactional Approach*. New York: Random House, 1954.

Jefferson, Margo. "Black Graffiti," *Newsweek*, July 21, 1975, 64–66.

Jencks, Christopher. *Rethinking Social Policy: Race, Poverty, and the Underclass.* New York: HarperPerennial, 1992.

Jhally, Sut, and Justin Lewis. *Enlightened Racism: The Cosby Show, Audiences, and the Myth of the American Dream.* Boulder, Colo.: Westview Press, 1992.

Jones, Jacquie. "The New Ghetto Aesthetic." *Wide Angle* 13, nos. 3–4 (July–October 1991): 32–43.

———. "Peer Pressure." *Black Film Review* 7, no. 2 (1993): 24.

King, Thomas R. "Advertising Campaign for Black Youth Film Spurs Fears of Violence." *Wall Street Journal*, January 13, 1992, sec. B, p. 6.

Kolbert, Elizabeth. "In the Race against Depravity." *New York Times*, June 5, 1995, sec. 4, p. 4.

Korzenny, Felipe, ed. *Mass Media Effects across Cultures.* London: Sage Publications, 1992.

Kuhn, Annette. *The Power of the Image: Essays on Representation and Sexuality.* Boston: Routledge, 1985.

———. "Women's Genres: Annette Kuhn Considers Melodrama, Soap Opera and Theory." *Screen* 25, no. 1 (1984): 18–28.

Lacayo, Richard. "Are Music and Movies Killing America's Soul?" *Time*, June 12, 1995, 25–30.

Landis, David, and Sally Ann Stewart. "Violence Doesn't Hurt 'Boyz' Gate." *USA Today*, July 15, 1991, A-1.

Leland, John, and Donna Foote. "A Bad Omen for Black Movies." *Newsweek*, July 29, 1991, 48–50.

Lembo, Ron, and Kathy Tucker. "Culture, Television, and Opposition: Rethinking Cultural Studies." *Critical Studies in Mass Communication* 7 (1990): 97–116.

Liebes, Tamar, and Elihu Katz. *The Export of Meaning: Cross-Cultural Readings of Dallas.* New York: Oxford University Press, 1990.

Light, Alan. "Not Just One of the Boyz." *Rolling Stone*, no. 612 (September 5, 1991): 73–75.

Lunt, Peter, and Sonia Livingstone. "Rethinking Focus Groups in Media and Communications Research." *Journal of Communication* 46, no. 2 (1996): 79–98.

Massood, Paula J. *Black City Cinema: African American Urban Experiences in Film.* Philadelphia: Temple University Press, 2003.

Mayne, Judith. *Cinema and Spectatorship.* New York: Routledge, 1993.

McLuhan, Marshall. *Understanding Media.* New York: Mentor Books, 1964.

Merton, Robert, Marjorie Fiske, and Patricia L. Kendall. *Focused Interview: A Manual of Problems and Procedures.* 2nd ed. New York: Free Press, 1990.

Monaco, James. *How to Read a Film: The Art, Technology, Language, History, and Theory of Film and Media.* New York: Oxford University Press, 1981.

Morgan, David. *Focus Groups as Qualitative Research.* Newbury Park, Calif.: Sage Publications, 1988.

Morley, David. *The Nationwide Audience: Structure and Decoding*. London: British Film Institute, 1980.

———. "Texts, Readers, Subjects." In *Culture, Media, Language*, edited by Stuart Hall, Dorothy Hobson, Andrew Lowe, and Paul Willis, 163–76. London: Hutchinson, 1980.

Mulvey, Laura. "Visual Pleasures in Narrative Cinema." In *Visual and Other Pleasures*, edited by Laura Mulvey, 14–26. Bloomington: Indiana University Press, 1989.

Mumby, Dennis. "Ideology and the Social Construction of Meaning: A Communication Perspective." *Communication Quarterly* 37 (1989): 291–304.

Murray, James P. "Lurid Movie Boom Over, but Black Films Steady On." *Variety*, January 7, 1975, 277: 16, 74.

———. "Reel Images—The Film Scene." *New York Amsterdam News*, July 20, 1974, D-16.

Office of Juvenile Justice and Delinquency Prevention. *Juveniles and Violence: Juvenile Offending and Victimization*, Fact Sheet #19. Washington, D.C.: Office of Juvenile Justice and Delinquency Prevention, November 1994.

Powell, Dantaun B. "Menace II Society or Product of Society?" *Washington Afro-American*, June 12, 1993, 87.

Prince, Gerald. "Introduction to the Study of the Narratee." In *Reader-Response Criticism*, edited by Jane P. Thompkins, 7–25. Baltimore: The Johns Hopkins University Press, 1980.

Purnima, Mankekar. *Screening Culture, Viewing Politics: An Ethnography of Television, Womanhood, and Nation in Postcolonial India*. Durham, N.C.: Duke University Press, 1999.

Radway, Janice. *Reading the Romance: Women, Patriarchy, and Popular Literature*. Chapel Hill: University of North Carolina Press, 1984.

Reid, Mark. *Redefining Black Film*. Berkeley: University of California Press, 1993.

Rhines, Jesse. *Black Film/White Money*. New Brunswick, N.J.: Rutgers University Press, 1996.

Rose, Tricia. *Black Noise: Rap Music and Black Culture in Contemporary America*. Hanover, N.H.: Wesleyan University Press, 1994.

Rosenblatt, Louise. *Literature as Exploration*. New York: D. Appleton-Century, 1938.

Seidman, Irving. E. *Interviewing as Qualitative Research*. New York: Teachers College Press, 1991.

Shively, JoEllen. "Cowboys and Indians: The Perception of Western Films among American Indians and Anglo Americans." Ph.D. diss., Stanford University, 1990.

———. "Cowboys and Indians: Perceptions of Western Films among American Indians and Anglos." *American Sociological Review* 57 (1992): 725–34.

Silverman, Kaja. *The Acoustic Mirror: The Female Voice in Psychoanalysis and Cinema*. Bloomington: Indiana University Press, 1988.

Smith, Angela E. "Two Fine Actors Inspire Youth in New Film" *New York Amsterdam News*, June 4, 1975, sec. B, p. 14.

Staiger, Janet. *Interpreting Films*. Princeton, N.J.: Princeton University Press, 1992.

Steiner, Linda. "Oppositional Decoding as an Act of Resistance." *Critical Studies in Mass Communication* 5, no. 1 (1988): 1–15.

Sterrit, David. "Streetwise Film *Juice* Stirs Up Bad Publicity." *Christian Science Monitor*, February 11, 1992, 11.

Stevenson, Richard W. "An Anti-Gang Movie Opens to Violence." *New York Times*, July 14, 1991, sec. 1, p. 10.

Thomas, Sari, ed. *Communication and Culture: Language Performance, Technology, and Media*. Norwood, N.J.: Ablex Publishing, 1990.

———. *Film/Culture: Explorations of Cinema in its Social Context*. Metuchen, N.J.: Scarecrow Press, 1982.

Tompkins, Jane, ed. *Reader-Response Criticism*. Baltimore: The John Hopkins University Press, 1980.

Turan, Kenneth. "L.A. Boyz Life: Growing Up in South Central—A Gritty *Boys n the Hood*." *Los Angeles Times*, July 12, 2001, F1, F6.

U.S. Bureau of the Census. "Poverty Thresholds in 1996, by Size of Family and Number of Related Children under 18 Years." Current Population Reports, Consumer Income Series P60-185. Washington, D.C.: U.S. Government Printing Office, 1996.

Van Deburg, William L. *Hoodlum: Black Villains and Social Bandits in American Life*. Chicago: University of Chicago Press, 2004.

Watkins, S. Craig. *Representing: Hip-Hop Culture and the Production of Black Cinema*. Chicago: University of Chicago Press, 1998.

Williamson, Judith. *Decoding Advertisements: Ideology and Meaning in Advertising*. London: Marion Boyars, 1978.

Wilson, Clint C., II, and Felix Gutierrez. *Minorities and Media: Diversity and the End of Mass Communication*. Beverly Hills, Calif.: Sage Publications, 1985.

Wilson, William, ed. *The Declining Significance of Race: From Racial Oppression to Economic Class Subordination*. Chicago: University of Chicago Press, 1976.

———. *The Ghetto Underclass: Social Science Perspectives*. Newbury Park, Calif.: Sage Publications, 1993.

Yearwood, Gladstone, ed. *Black Cinema Aesthetics*. Athens: Ohio University Press, 1982.

~

Index

~

About the Author

Celeste A. Fisher holds a Ph.D. in culture and communication. She sits on the advisory board of *Inter-Cultural Studies*, a journal of social change and cultural diversity, and has been a special issue editor for the *International Journal of Media and Cultural Politics*. She teaches film and media studies in New York City.